alms for oblivion

ESSAYS BY EDWARD DAHLBERG

with a foreword by Sir Herbert Read

University of Minnesota Press, Minneapolis

Library of Congress Catalog Card Number: 64-13767

PUBLISHED IN GREAT BRITAIN, INDIA, AND PAKISTAN BY THE OXFORD UNIVERSITY PRESS
LONDON, BOMBAY, AND KARACHI, AND IN CANADA BY THOMAS ALLEN, LTD., TORONTO

For Julia Lawlor, County Cavan, Ireland

FOREWORD

I REMEMBER that early in my career as a writer an unknown well-wisher wrote and begged me to give up my critical activities and confine myself to the kind of literature for which my gifts were better suited, namely, imaginative literature. I was told I had an eye for concrete particulars and little ability in philosophical generalizations. I was reminded of this admonition when I read the first pages of Edward Dahlberg's essay on Allen Tate, for there he describes, if only obliquely, his own practice in criticism. It appears that he too has no love and perhaps little gift for "the mock elevated style of the philosopher and scientist," and yet this essay, and all the rest that comprise this volume, are nothing if not critical. We may therefore conclude that there are at least two methods of criticism. One we might call philosophical and the other, if a philosophical critic had not usurped the term, practical. Since practical criticism as a descriptive phrase has come to be associated with those "sophisters" and "noddies" who attempt "to find out what is in the poet's mind as he labors for precise numbers," we cannot very well use it to define Edward

Dahlberg's kind of criticism (which is also the kind of Ben Jonson, Dryden, and Bagehot). I would call it "concrete" criticism, but Mr. Dahlberg would say that such a word belongs to "the jargon of aesthetics." His preference is to speak of auricular and sensual pleasures, and literature must first and foremost satisfy his "goatish appetite" for such phenomenal fodder. The pose is Gargantuan, and Rabelais is undoubtedly one of our author's monitors. Like Rabelais, he will list a hundred particulars, but never risk a generalization. It is not possible to define pleasure or truth. "Since knowledge is chimerical, the academic stench is more horrid when the cabala of grammar is passed off as metaphysics." Since Mr. Dahlberg despises so many academic ideals — definition, analysis, syntax, the scientific method itself — it is little wonder that he is not honored in Academe, which is to say, not in any hall of renown, for nowadays they are all leased to pedants.

Mr. Dahlberg would describe himself merely as a humble reader, "rapt in love with" poetry and prose. His criticism when it ceases to be denunciatory, is confession. Some of the best of his pages are memories, and he would say that because style is the man himself, a knowledge of the man is a key to his style. His portraits of Dreiser, Anderson, and Ford Madox Ford tell us more about these authors, as authors, than a whole library of exegesis. Even the glimpse of Allen Tate's "wry, Poesque face flensed by some teleological anguish," tells us more about Tate's genius than the preceding references to his works. He does not write many words about Edmund Wilson or William Carlos Williams, but those words bite deeply and are indelible.

I should perhaps emulate the author's method in this tribute, but I doubt my skill. I have known him many years, in his joy and his suffering, and count myself lucky to have retained his respect and love, for he is a relentless scourge of all human frailties, especially those that threaten the integrity of the writer. He tells us (in this book) that what our genius lacks most is being simple, and though he is as ever thinking of style, the style is not separable from the way of life. He himself has always preferred to live simply, and his dwellings have been like the hermit's cell. I do not imply loneliness or lack of human contacts, for he enjoys good talk, despises the pervert, and believes that bad writing shows a lack of love. A poet, he says, "comes to the city to get his thoughts published, but there is always in him some wild Platte Dakota, or Rocky Mountain peak to resist the simpering vices of trade and deceit. Writing is conscience, scruple, and the farming of our ancestors." Typical that he should add this last phrase, but a poet concerned for style is likely to have a stronger sense of social values than the styleless sociologue. This poet believes (as I do) that "unless we return to the old handicrafts, to the wheat, stable, and horse village, to poems, houses, bricks, and tables, which are manual, we will become a nation of killers, for if people do not employ their hands in making what is good, or gentle, or noble, they will be criminals." Edward Dahlberg's criticism is a protest against our universal condition of alienation, which is our condition of damnation, and it is little wonder that the damned turn away from its revelation of their condition.

Sunset, he says on another page, "has fallen upon American letters, though it is less than a hundred years ago that we had a meadowy, daybreak verse and essay. It looked as though we were on the verge of some unusual sunrise; the land was pasture; Thoreau's *Walden* was a woodland lesson and prayer in how to live without wasting the human spirit." Those moving words give us the essence of the man and his message. Here, as everywhere, he fulfills his own ideal — his style is another name for his perception and his wisdom.

That perception and that wisdom culminate in the most direct and surprising contradiction of accepted values in his essay on Melville. I confess I had always shared the common admiration for Melville's allegorical epic, but never was an illusion of mine so immediately shattered. Of course, many American critics will come to the rescue of a work of such decisive import for the myth of an American literature, but Mr. Dahlberg takes his stand on what is most central to literature of any kind, the language, and he has no difficulty in showing that *Moby-Dick* is "shabbily written." He makes concessions, to the style as well as to social relevance, but in the end there is no escaping the conclusion that *Moby-Dick* is "a book of monotonous and unrelenting gloom." The gloom would not matter, and the monotony is relieved by such miraculous images as the one rescued from the gloom by Mr. Dahlberg himself —"the currents carry ye to those sweet Antilles where the beaches are only beat with water-lilies." It is conceded that Melville had enough genius to sing on occasion (our author cites a further litany of "canorous lines"), but they are not enough to save Melville's vessel from the weight of his indignation.

It should be noted, however, that this indignation is fundamentally moral. What Mr. Dahlberg objects to most strongly in Melville is his misogamy. "There is no doxy, trollop, or trull in any of Melville's volumes . . . The hatred of women is the pederastic nausea that comes from the mention of the womb . . . Melville, Whitman, Poe, and Thoreau loathed the female, and the first three sages suffered from sodomy of the heart." Such intellectual sodomy ("as gross and abundant today as sexual perversion") is the burden of much of Edward Dahlberg's criticism, and it comes from his conviction that such "pathic" elements in modern literature come from "the refusal to be simple about plain matters." We return, therefore, to the test of style, and by always returning to this test, by insisting on very little else, Mr. Dahlberg becomes a critic of a most salutary kind. His judgments are severe, but they are motivated by a conviction he shares with Henry James, namely, "the very obvious truth that the deepest quality of a work of art will always be the quality of the mind of the producer." The moral sense and the artistic sense, as James observed on the same occasion, lie very near together, and it is Edward Dahlberg's distinction, in an age that has largely forgotten, if it ever heeded this admonition, to have reminded us of its obvious truth.

HERBERT READ

September 9, 1963

TABLE OF CONTENTS

alms for oblivion

MY FRIENDS
STIEGLITZ, ANDERSON, AND DREISER

I HAVE NOT KNOWN TWELVE GOOD MEN — plain, honest Galilean fishermen of the soul — but I have been the familiar of twelve talented ones. Alfred Stieglitz, to whom seven or eight volumes of fine writing were dedicated, had genius, but he was not a good man. We are so double in our values that it is necessary to say this. An artist should have some kind of single personality and there ought to be a oneness about a book or a deed; but faces, writing, and acts are no longer very reliable.

Stieglitz had the most gifted countenance I have seen and it was always an artistic pleasure to look at his eyes, brown as those of the cow-goddess Io; he had a good brow (we know that Plato in Greek means wide forehead) and his square chin was like an example out of Euclid. Schopenhauer believed that the face always divulged the nature of the man, though he also realized that it required a soothsayer's ability not to misjudge it. The aged Priam of ruined Troy satiated his heart as he contemplated Achilles. When he knelt in supplication he knew that he was kissing manslaughtering hands; as he gazed at the ravening lion of Greece we are not sure what he saw. After Stieglitz removed his glasses one expected to find in those deep orbs the compassion of Isaiah's pools of Heshbon. I think he suffered from what has been called man's most malignant affliction, coldness. Genius can be cold too, and often is, but there is a dragon, a sphynx that is half-virgin and half-beast, in frigid art. I say all this not to appear complex or to make more human riddles than there already are. But Alfred Stieglitz baffled me, and I am sure that he did not understand himself very well; I believe that people who are as unreliable as he was are not at the essentials of them simple as Christ or Jeremiah. A prophet learned his trade and he went about his business of being a seer — you always knew where you were with him; you can be a friend of a man or a book when you understand the relationship between you and the person or the book.

I have observed writing people a great deal; I recall how perplexed I was the first time Sherwood Anderson came to see Stieglitz. Then past middle age and sick, Stieglitz used to lie on an austere barracks cot in a whited alcove that opened out to An American Place at 509 Madison Avenue, where exhibits of Marsden Hartley, Dove, O'Keeffe, and Marin were given. He had been told some years before to go home and die, or wait for death, but he was very impatient and had turned this little monastery-alcove into an open sepulchre. Lots of people, like Dreiser and Ford Madox Ford, said he was senile and obviously mad. He was as repetitious as older men can be, and as the young are. There was only one mark of dotage that I ever observed in him: he played with his handkerchief just as fatuously as decrepit Lear might have done, or as Dreiser himself did. Sherwood Anderson was much kinder to Dreiser than Dreiser was to Stieglitz, and one remembers with the most agreeable feelings Anderson's tribute to old Dreiser playing with his handkerchief in *Horses and Men*. Stieglitz used to lie on the spartan army cot with his hand on his bad heart as though he looked into his grave all day long, like Donne.

Had I not seen Stieglitz's photograph of Anderson, the Ohio populist and sex rebel, with the midland bangs of hair, I don't think I would have paid much attention to the man sitting on a stool in the alcove and speaking in a drawl. He was wearing purple socks, a shiny brown store suit, store teeth, and his throat had a loose sick hang to it. Stieglitz never bothered to introduce me to him. He was a crank about such matters and thought that people ought to make things happen themselves. He had established 291 for his disciples of the arts, but sometimes he acted as though he wanted to keep them apart. He was full of these crotchety intuitions about the deportment of everybody.

I found Anderson in the first meeting a far from piercing human being; even Dreiser was less commonplace looking than this human platitude that had warmed many fine books and women. One never knows where genius is; in the hands, the trembling fingers. In Ezekiel the Angel has a dove in one cheek and in the other a predatory eagle. Sherwood Anderson had, as I later saw, hot brown eyes, and what was most revealing in Stieglitz were his wrists. Many looked at the crazy clumps of hair that grew out of his ears like satyr's horns, but this was artistic show, his gaudy affront to the philistines. He had doll-like wrists that were as fluent and feminine as Lawrence's. Stieglitz was an astonishing little doll of the arts, but one fondles a doll rather than loves it, and everyone that came to see Stieglitz wooed and caressed his moods, which were as unstable as water. Except for John Marin, the watercolorist, I don't think he cared for anyone. Marin was the only artist he never maligned; he hated Hartley, whom he had helped for thirty years, and he showed Hartley, a remarkable painter, to have the heart of a *flaneur* in that photograph he made of him. Marsden Hartley was an uglified dandy of the arts; he was the superlative male bitch artist of his day, and perhaps the best painter America has ever produced. A species of cyclops, one could neither love nor like him; Hartley had a titanic, swollen head, almost no mouth, and a voracious, orgiastic nose. Baffling enough, he had a satanic intellect that was always writhing on the cross.

Stieglitz was a little D. H. Lawrence talking like Buddha. He spoke as D. H. Lawrence wrote: he kept on talking until he said something good, just as Lawrence continued to write until he blundered into an amazing intuition. Stieglitz and Lawrence were intuitive, automatic people; if you

5]

listened to Stieglitz long enough you would hear a gnomic remark, and it might take you as long as to read the first two hundred dull pages of a Lawrence novel, but both ordeals were worth the patience. Many called him a bore because he said the same things so many times, but this was the charge brought against Socrates by quibblers and enemies. I like a man to have a little of the easy, relaxed bore about him; it is a comfort to the soul and gives peace to the bowels to hear a good man say good things often. One of my main objections to Alfred Stieglitz was this: his conduct was not boring enough. He was, as I have said, a waterseer, like Proteus, the Nile prophet with whom Menelaus had to grapple and who kept changing from a river whale to a shaggy water camel, and Polonius is the same sort of person; the pocketbook sage, to avoid raising Hamlet's choler, is willing to admit that the cloud looks like a lion or a waterhog. It is not how clever a man is that endears him to us, but how stable is his nature. Goethe once said of Byron that he was not a poet but a nature, and this is what I imagine Dostoevski was. Whatever he did or what book he wrote his acts appear to me to be a part of a whole, virtuous man.

Stieglitz was a chameleon in his affections. Sometimes he would attack a friend because he himself felt old, rancid, and already coffined. On one occasion he railed at Hartley because the latter had been sitting on a wooden stool in the burial alcove for hours. "He won't move!" exclaimed Stieglitz, almost beside himself; but Marsden Hartley was not only motionless, he was also deaf. When Stieglitz was not thinking about art, he was obsessed with death, and Hartley considered the one almost as fatal as the other; art was always mixed with death. When a woman praised Hartley's show at the Walker gallery the artist replied: "My paintings ought to be good; I'm just about ready to be cremated." In this moody, irascible family of geniuses, one could not be sure of anyone. There was William Carlos Williams who came to the Place, and who wrote a very fine essay in a very bad book called *America and Alfred Stieglitz*. The late Paul Rosenfeld, another acolyte, who had helped O'Keeffe and Anderson, was flighty, feminine. I remember Waldo Frank, a bombastic cherub, rushing into the arms of Stieglitz who stepped back with congealed composure, causing me to rebuke him afterwards. I told Stieglitz I thought that art and literature were for human love. Though Waldo Frank had unusual sensibilities, he had hardly any sense of judgment, and Stieglitz, the greatest art peacock in America, had scant use for the great Frank who was such an art hen about his books.

Frank was one of the initial criers for the brave Randolph Bourne, the discerning friend of the poet Hart Crane, and the first to appreciate Anderson's *Winesburg, Ohio*. Anderson and Frank had been good friends. Frank told Anderson that the world's greatest writers were Joyce, Anderson, and Waldo Frank, and then when Anderson made one of his sententious midwestern replies, "Waldo, if you don't cut out that I am great stuff, I won't see you any more," Waldo wept. After some reassuring words from Anderson they went out for a walk and Frank burst forth with "Sherwood, Europe is waiting for us."

Two things destroyed Frank as a writer: the grossest vanity and the adjective. I think he might have written a remarkable book had he not been so greedy to be known by everybody (for he always had the neck of a crane for fame); and had he not always used an adjective for a verb, which makes for a feminine sentence. There ought to be a strong man in a sentence, to make it active rather than passive; we are astonished by Homer because he writes as Achilles casts the spear of Pelion ash. Every verb should have that epical and martial force.

Stieglitz had said many times that he did not like the word "artist"— that if a man painted or wrote it was his own fault. He often fell into the most destructive nihilism about literature and painting, saying that he hated art and that he intended to burn all his photographs, for great as his faults were he could perceive them most plainly — in others. Once when he was wallowing in the role of Timon, hating everybody, Williams became very choleric and told him to go home and die, that his sniveling melancholia was murdering everyone at the Place. Williams was right, but hardly the man to rebuke him, being himself a ravine and cold-water man. Williams was a provincial pill-satchel man of Rutherford, New Jersey. He was a doctor perhaps because he looked all his life for human staples, for direct potato-and-apple people, with simple arithmetic morals and plain salt and pepper in their acts. Art people today have not honest bread, pear, and chicory or grass in their vices, deeds, and souls, and Williams, the genius of *In the American Grain*, had as much loose water in his nature as there was in Stieglitz.

When Stieglitz was in good fettle as a seer, and sure of his animal intuitions, he would call out as I stepped into the alcove, "Just when you opened the door, Sherwood's *Many Marriages* fell off the top shelf. I said 'that is a neglected book and that's Dahlberg, a neglected man, coming in.' " After Stieglitz had talked till dusk he said, "We've had a rare talk today; you must come soon again." Although I had seldom been successful in interrupting him, what he said was the truth; the best conversation between two persons is a monologue, the art that Alfred Stieglitz knew best.

Stieglitz had a passion for white. An American Place was a white sepulchre — his East River penthouse reminded me of the albic tunic Melville said the Leviathan, Moby-Dick, wore. Georgia O'Keeffe, his wife, had the same mania for Hygeia, the old, sanitary goddess who ruled so many of her paintings in the Stieglitz-O'Keeffe apartment. Against the white apartment walls were the bleached cow skull, the tombed lilies, and the frigid vulva flowers.

One night at the East River penthouse Stieglitz was in his prophetic season, and he said to me with the greatest gravity and in the Hebrew meter of Genesis, "In my entire life I have entered twelve women; I am seventy-five, and still very potent." He spoke like the law-giver writing how Abraham went in unto Hagar, and this was said with such patriarchic purity that I thought of Enos and Methuselah who lived when there were no feeble men on the earth, for otherwise Methuselah's long years must have been a curse rather than a blessing, particularly the last eight hundred and thirty years or so. The Psalmist tells us that after seventy all is sorrow and affliction and impotency. Of course, I don't know any more about Methuselah than I did about Alfred Stieglitz, who may have been lying;

but then all good storytellers, like Stieglitz, Anderson, and Ford Madox Ford, were marvelous liars.

Once when Stieglitz was raving wildly about Georgia O'Keeffe's paintings, he showed me his photographs of her hands — large hands, with fierce knuckles and punishing fingers which somehow resembled the face of Savonarola, and I told him so. He nodded with rare enthusiasm and took out more camerawork he had done on her hands. Stieglitz, no less than Aristotle and Turgeniev, had to be whipped by women; he was unusually fond of women, up till the last, for one chit who went to see him after he was eighty said he had wonderful, prehensile hands. Virginia Woolf would have called this fingering lewdness. All of these people of An American Place were sex geniuses, but lacked the stuff out of which are made the sorrowful windmill visions and Sancho-Panza laughs and the great erotical sports of the *Sonnets*.

I mistook Ford the first time for one of the pigs Circe had fed with acorns and masts. He had a large, loafy face, and he used to shamble fatly down Eighth Street, slowly fetching air. He had two rooms at number 10 Fifth Avenue, a brownstone across from the old Brevoort Hotel, and gave Thursday afternoon tea and talk. Ford was insanely kind and his gray eyes were warm oracles. Ford lied about everything; he said that he never looked up one quotation for his *March of Literature*. His belly, loosely suspendered, so that his obese trousers were always below his navel, shook when he cited some early English writer, Izaak Walton, or White, who had written that birds "copulate on the wing," or contended that all of Shakespeare's plays were potboilers except *Timon of Athens*. Who would have imagined that there was a darkling vein of Timon in such portly, good-natured blood? One day he told me, with the utmost affected confidence, that he believed most of the Americans were impotent. Yet I never knew anybody who thought American writing was so puissant and important as he did. His kindness was a wind that was always blowing his head about in one direction or another. He simply could not do enough for our talented authors. He also lied about his southern manor to which he invited everybody he liked — and he had the fattest affections for people — but there was no manor. Then, when he first met Stieglitz, Ford said he was crazy! Sherwood Anderson, whose autobiographical books are plain, honest perjury, said that he was very fond of Ford, although he was a preposterous liar.

Both Ford and Anderson were sex visionaries and they understood people because they touched them. Touch is our misery, our disgrace and our knowledge. In John it is said that the truthseeker is without pity, but that the sensual man sorrows for others. This profound observation explains Sherwood Anderson, who did not have a great head, but whose flesh was always growing and ripening for others. I think that Anderson was the man Whitman adumbrated for us in his astounding manifesto on physiology, *Leaves of Grass*. Nobody in this country has ever been so close to Isaiah's "All flesh is grass" as Anderson, for his skin was as nervous and touchy as grass is in the sun, and he had to cohabit with every woman in his books, whether she was Helen or the hag Hecuba, because he was entirely sympathetic. He told me that one day Edgar Lee Masters' fiancee came to him weeping, "Edgar won't marry me," and that he had put his arms around her and said, "Don't cry, darling, I'll wed you," and he did.

His aching skin took the place of what we others call mind, but which is more important than the human brain, because it is infinitely more loving. One does not have to be afraid of a meadow, which won't hurt you; what is to be dreaded is the mind without feeling, for it is a most malignant faculty. Anderson had a large respect for Dreiser, thinking of him as someone big with child, who, when he conceived, brought forth a monster, the USA Titan, that has assaulted Zeus and the heavens for lightning and atomic bombs. God take away our powers and give us instead the grass in Sherwood Anderson.

Anderson told me on Christmas at Marion, Virgina, but without malice, "This is the way Teddy writes: 'It was a dark, inky, mizzling, misty night; in fact, it was a terrible rainy night.'" He said that Dreiser had to swear whenever he was amorous, which tells us a lot about Mollie Bloom's four-letter words in *Ulysses* and the obscenities in *Lady Chatterley's Lover*.

Anderson cowered before money, fearing it might destroy what was fecund in him. When he was in New Orleans, the publisher Horace Liveright asked him to write a novel, offering him a hundred and twenty-five dollars a week while he was working at it. Anderson, who had run away from an Ohio wife and a paint factory because money had become a sign of impotency to him, agreed. He told me with his midland guitar twang "I had forgotten how to spend money like that, and soon the $125 checks began to overlap, and I grew cold and unable whenever I looked at those bank certificates." When Liveright came to see him, he asked, "What's the matter, Sherwood, you look so gloomy; has somebody offered you $150 a week for the book?" "No," replied Anderson, "that's not it; but Horace, you've got to stop sending me all that money, those checks are killing me, I can't write." Liveright then sent Anderson a modest weekly sum and Anderson wrote the one book, *Dark Laughter*, out of which he made money — lucre that was the source of wife and house trouble for Anderson. One of his wives wanted him to build a fancy house, and he did, somewhere near Marion, Virginia, paying the workmen such good wages that the people in the town were bitter in their complaints: they said that before he had come there was none of that northern city dollar discontent in Marion. To begin with, Anderson had gone to Marion to be humble and to get away from money, which separates people. There is a very fine example of this dollar-fear in *Poor White*. Hugh McVey, who has become a rich Ohio inventor, is afraid of his nuptial night and runs away from his bride. He had been a desolate railroad depot telegrapher, and then had grown wealthy by inventing a grass-seeding device. He, who taught the farmers how to plant in the shortest time, was afraid to seed his own bride.

Sherwood Anderson never got over his money-fear, any more than his friend Dreiser did. Dreiser is the greatest dollar genius of the American novel. The best interpretation of any of his books is the Mount Kisco mansion he had, which resembled a Log Cabin syrup can. He had a luxurious writing table made out of an airplane wing, and in his heyday he went to parties with a pair of autocratic Russian hounds. Everybody in a Dreiser novel wants dollars; Sister Carrie sacrifices Hurstwood for money, and the carriagemaker gives up Jennie Gerhardt because should he marry her, he would then have only ten thousand a year. Cowperwood, who is really Yerkes the capitalist, in *The Financier* and *The Titan*, is only creative when his brain is boiling and scheming for new fortunes.

Dreiser was an extraordinary business novelist who dismissed Stieglitz as a crank because hair grew out of his ears. He had vehement barbershop morals, and, regarding my long hair with a merchant's suspicion, advised a haircut. He was much more reflective than his books. Teaching me how to read Shakespeare, he said that all the plays were man-eating parables, and that life rather than the poet had written the tragedies. He was always rewriting Ecclesiastes — rather badly — and he had unusual emotions about the Sermon on the Mount. One night he got very testy with me when I would not agree that the song "Annie Rooney" was as good as a Beethoven symphony. When he became somewhat ill-natured, I reminded him of Matthew's Sermon, and, laughing, he said, "Ho, let's go and see some girls." His women were girls that looked like boys — at least those that I saw — and I wondered about these breastless, skinny college hoydens. Our women in beribboned curls and skirts to their knees dress up like little children to whet the appetite of the men.

One afternoon on a Central Park bench Dreiser told me that he was getting his convictions into order. He said that he had seen a fair-haired boy in the park and had come to appreciate the Greek's preference for men. This astonished and troubled me, and I wondered why this large masculine figure, seldom wrapped in a winter overcoat, had come so to think. Although his face was something like a dry gourd, he had a smile that must have enfeebled the will of many women, so these were not the words of a hungry man.

Masculine will has greatly dwindled and we are producing feminine verse and literature. Billy Budd is really a Greek boy like the late Hart Crane. It is the mother that dominates American literature. Dreiser, who was in temperament an anarchist, may have become a communist because his mother was an Indiana Mennonite, a member of a religious communistic sect that had its origins in Martin Luther's Germany. We have a

Mother Literature, and the male parent in our verse and novel is very weak. Melville's father is far in the rear, ineffectual, as we see in *Pierre*, and in Whitman it is the Quaker mother with whose image he was connected. Poe and all the men in the tales are wan. And who fathered desolate, seagoing Ahab, moaning for a bed, the marriage pillow, a dry family hearse? We are making a homeless culture, for there is no one to father the household. There is no hearth in Thoreau, Poe, or Melville, or celibate Whitman, and we never see people at table in their books. There is no bread in a hempen basket, a flagon of claret, or a chine of beef in Marsden Hartley, O'Keeffe, Marin, Dove, or a remarkable Stieglitz photograph.

Dreiser, Stieglitz, Hartley were fatherless men, without the essential masculine force to love people. Dreiser had a hard, craggy apathy toward people, and Stieglitz's passion was as refrigerated as O'Keeffe's paintings. Stieglitz was exceedingly generous, but not tender, and he was entirely sympathetic with the economic problems of a painter. Still, he rather detested the artist. Very vain himself, he loathed anybody who laureled his own canvas or book. He was as nihilistic and outrageous as Lear; he had the opportunity to reveal to me that when his mother was cremated he had no feelings about it at all. Maybe he was attempting to astonish me, but I have learned that whatever a man tells you about himself is true, even though it is a lie. Stieglitz had the exquisite feminine sensibility to resist, but he had not the will to resist enough which makes great male art. Like Socrates, he questioned everything, asking the most random gallery visitor what he meant when he used the word justice or love; but unlike the sage at Athens, he said that justice and love did not exist, and when a man says that he eats his own prayers and strivings.

He did not set aside human ends, although in fits of melancholia he often destroyed them. Whenever a young, raw, apprentice painter told him he wanted to become an artist, Stieglitz asked the enthusiast in the iciest tone, "Are you ready to starve?" and if the youth faltered in his reply, he sent him away. When Marsden Hartley was an obscure Maine artist he asked Stieglitz to show his work, declaring that he could live on four dollars a week. That was enough for Stieglitz, who exhibited Hartleys in his various galleries for thirty years.

That whole generation of artseekers was not so sick as we are. Dreiser had none of that being-busy malady; he had time for his writing kindred, and he never put you off by telling you that he was either beginning a novel or finishing one. He had none of that wordsickness in his soul, and any adjective he might lose one day he was certain to recover the next. Stieglitz ran open shop at the Place for conversation; fat, gracious Ford was as hospitable as Zeus, and would beg you to come for tea and to bring along some early or late book you had written so he could find out whether you were a quack or not.

Whenever I pass the 10 Fifth Avenue brownstone my steps fumble a little and I think of Ford's eyes, the dove-gray eyes of the Shulamite, as Lawrence described them. They were amorous eyes, soft and almost wet, because they were always feeling something. All these droll, perceiving natures died at about the same time — first Ford, then Anderson and Hartley and Dove, and then Dreiser.

Somehow or other the whole literature and painting movement is the fable of Alfred Stieglitz, the little figure in black pancake hat and gypsy cape. Almost everybody at one time or another was in Stieglitz's gallery, and he was the crazy art-autocrat of them all. He was not only the angel that foolishly rushed in where others feared to tread; he had no fear afterwards of being mocked, either. He brought Cézanne over when New Yorkers jeered at that master's work; he was one of the first of D. H. Lawrence's readers, buying his wonderful small volume on our literature by the dozen when criticasters like Van Wyck Brooks and Edmund Wilson said it was a hoax. I mean Lawrence's *Studies in Classical American Literature*. When Stieglitz cared for a book he bought two or three dozen of them to hand out to friends or prospective followers.

Stieglitz was a doting-mad camera man, and he refused ten thousand dollars for Steichen's photograph of J. P. Morgan, which he offered to the Metropolitan for nothing, provided they would hang it alongside Rembrandt. They wouldn't and he called them great boors of philistia. Stieglitz was a quacksalver as well as a sage; doubtless there is a charlatan in every savant. He was the first to demand outlandish and immoral prices for American art. That he did not make a penny out of the sale of a painting does not make his error the leaner. When a woman hesitated to buy a Dove, an O'Keeffe, or a Hartley he would urge her to go home and think it over for a year or two. He would say: "It may be that you and art are not quite compatible with one another; for instance, if there is the least amount of marital strife in your household, a Hartley could easily disturb the sexual relations between you and your husband. However, there is no connubial sedative as good as a Marin. Come back one year from today when the sun is in Aries."

Those who have known the sorrows of penury will eulogize Stieglitz for what he did; but there is no reason why a painter or a writer should be paid more than a porter or a charwoman; that he is given less than either is a part of our occidental idiocy and waste. No matter; it is just as ridiculous to ask $5,000 for a Marin as it would be to demand that much money for a sonnet. He was full of the most trifling paradoxes. He declared that he hated America and then named his gallery An American Place. He would remark that this is the cruelest land in the world for the artist, but maintain that a Marin seawash was American. He insisted on a kind of biblical USA geography in art.

Alfred Stieglitz was the most exquisite of all heart-wounders. The people he hurt most came to kiss his hand as he lay on the alcove cot or to press the fragile tortoise-shell wrists, and to bless him for making them whole. Everybody fondled him because people were already orphans in the big-cold street nation. Stieglitz was a father and mother doll for the literature and painting orphans who had no playthings besides their books and canvases, and no one to love. Alfred Stieglitz, who died in 1946, danced before Art in a white stole, like David at the Ark.

MIDWESTERN FABLE

THE INK PUNDITS OF OUR COLLEGES and the grammar boys of the magazines do not have the animal health to understand or even to smell the American midwest. Anderson's life is a fable of the old rural, wooden midwest, land of fine trees, sunflowers, and highgrass towns and streets. Anderson's father had a harness shop in Camden, Ohio, and when the family fell into inconvenient, but not immodest, want, his mother took in washing. Poverty was not sick and dirty and brutal, but was still warm, like noondays, and there was energy in the washtub, the porch steps, and the dandelions. Like other Ohio boys, Anderson sold newspapers (the *Cincinnati Enquirer*) to help his parents. By the time he was a full-grown man and had acquired a wife and three children, he was managing a paint factory in Elyria. There was a legend that Anderson had a trunk filled with short stories and novels. One morning, while dictating a letter to a stenographer, he paused, got his hat, and said: "Now I'm going out to walk on the dry bedrock of a river." Another story about Anderson the businessman was that whenever he wrote, his wife plaintively reproached him: "Oh, Sherwood, you're writing those tales again; are you trying to make paupers of your family?" Whatever shortcomings there were in his biography he healed by inventing tales and incidents that may have taken place only in his mind. He took sick, left his wife and children and the paint factory, and in a gypsy fit of amnesia he wandered to Cleveland, where he pretended that he was an artist.

A poet necessarily lies about everything, and the first falsehood he invents is that he is an artist. The Anderson hegira to Cleveland, away from his wife and the paint business, was also a song in Anderson's brain, "I'm a poet, a fine cobbler of singing words," and it was lucky for Anderson and for America that Harry Hansen knew how to hear this chanting nature.

Anderson became a Chicago copywriter and also the dude-artist, wearing hot, tropical ties, spats, and carrying a cane as he went down Michigan Avenue. He had read some George Moore, Thomas Hardy, and Turgeniev, and he spelled badly. He wanted to go to New York to meet the culture people and learn to be a better speller, but instead of Socrates and Diogenes he met Paul Rosenfeld and Waldo Frank.

Anderson did not have the speculative intellect of a Plato, but he had the natural integrity of a fine elm, or a fertile sow, or a potato; he had a burly, carnal mind which was always very close to his urgent, lustful hands and nose, and his books he begat, rather than wrote. Stieglitz made a marvelous photograph of the midland genius, with his bangs of hair (almost like those of Gertrude Stein, whom he admired and imitated) and his mouth, which was voluptuous like a woman's.

Along with Dreiser, Anderson had a great distrust of the mind. Once Tolstoi told Gorki not to read much because it would harm his genius, and I think he would have said the same to Dreiser or Anderson. Books were necessary for Melville, but had Anderson been a greater reader he would have overeaten.

Anderson had a manual intelligence: he had large, animal hands, like a peasant's, and all his wisdom was in his fingers. That is why he hated the machine, which can make the hands stupid and morose. A workman turning a wheel all day long in a factory will lose patience with ordinary life; indeed, much of human kindness comes from being casual and slow. Anderson was no hurried man; he had time to shake hands, make friendships, or engage in a mettlesome argument. Once we had a rather truculent conversation about Thomas Wolfe, whom he admired, at an Eighth Street bar and food place; and toward the fag-end of a querulous afternoon he paused, looking up at me like an uncertain woman who wants to know whether she is still loved, saying, "You think you know more than I do?" I had read much more than Anderson, but I cannot tell whether books have brought me closer to things or separated me from them. Besides, nobody knows more than a poet; even when an artist is factually wrong, his feelings may be right and true.

One day, sauntering past Sixth Avenue at Forty-fourth Street and looking at the wicked herd of cars and the mass of unseeing people who reminded me of those suffering shades that Dante says crossed a river with unwet feet, I said to Anderson, "Think with what malice New York has been conceived." He replied in that drawling midland voice, "Naw, it just happened." We were also talking about Dostoevski, and he said, "I don't want to suffer like Dostoevski." There is something sordid about happiness, and the avoidance of sorrow is pusillanimous. In spite of all the feeling I have for Sherwood Anderson, I never respected this cowardice in him. "Suffer, O Lord, or die," says St. Theresa. He wrote me some wrangling letters about Thomas Wolfe continuing our previous argument, and one day he asked me out of his uncertainty, "Do you believe *Bottom Dogs* is better than *Winesburg*?" I replied, "It is much less than *Winesburg*." In the meantime, after having seen two advertisements, adjacent to each other, in a Fifth Avenue bus, one of Thomas Wolfe's *Of Time and the River* and the other for Gulden's mustard, I was positive I was right. I had never read a line by Wolfe, but I do not have to read every bad book to assail it.

He was very unsure of himself; that is why he was never in a hurry with anybody, for it takes a long time to understand — or to misunderstand — people. He never had the American "busy" malady. Nor had Dreiser; if you wanted to see him, he always asked you to come over right away. Marsden Hartley was not fancy or affected either, until Paul Rosenberg, the art dealer, had sold thirty thousand dollars' worth of his work one year. Hartley told me the following story: At a literary party a Broadway theater magnate rushed into Hartley's arms, crying out with rapture: "Oh Marsden, we have not seen each other for twenty years; when shall we have dinner together?" To which Hartley replied: "Well, when?" That dumbfounded the Broadway impresario: "You know, Hartley, I have so many appointments, and by the weekend I must go to Connecticut to restore my flagging energies. This coming week is quite full, really overflowing; let me see about the next week after that; there's Monday, Tuesday, Wednesday, Thursday, Friday, and then, O God, another Connecticut weekend; what about three weeks from next Thursday?" Hartley, the flinty Maine artist, retorted: "Nothing doing; nobody is that busy." After which the theater man said rather sheepishly: "Would you please have dinner with me tonight?" Once I asked Alfred Stieglitz about Waldo Frank, and he answered, "Waldo's busy being great." Sherwood Anderson was never the great or the quick, and neither was Dreiser. I deeply wish that Sherwood Anderson were alive just to know that someone in America still has time to drink a bottle of wine and to talk, for until we have some good, slow people again we won't have books that enlarge our affections and trust.

The way to understand a man like Anderson is not to read about him but to read him. Reading him, you find that all those workinghand words of his are redolent of hay and grass and midwest stables. Get *Winesburg, Ohio*, or *Poor White*, or *Tar*, or the *Notebook*, or his still unrecognized verse, *A New Testament* and *Mid-American Chants*. Anderson's books have the heady pollen of good orchards. Aristotle says that the pleasure we take in smelling apples is good, but that an interest in unguents is a sign of debauchery. All you need is a healthy nose, for we smell good and evil much quicker than we understand them. Remembering old-style American habits, the lumbering wagon hello, and the easy country-morning how-do-you-do, is enough to make one understand Sherwood Anderson's genius, which is a compact of goodness and of love and of a patient willingness to sit and talk with people.

WORD-SICK AND PLACE-CRAZY

BOOKS ARE WILD BEASTS or brackish water or dead ravines. It is hard now to find a book that one can depend upon, and in which branch is bough, bird is bird, and apple talks like apple. Books are more mixed and dirty than ever, and though there is rot and swinepen in every poet, the old Levitical differences between fungused places and unclean froggish things and the arbute and gillyflower are gone. There is so much lion and jackal mischief in our morals, and man at best, as Hamlet says, is indifferent honest, that the poet is no longer homely and plain about simple and plain things. He is like William Carlos Williams, the Paterson rock poet, who gives us skill and invention in the place of the Cana marriage wine. His original books are Medusa's, likely to turn the heads of a generation into stone, and *Paterson* and *The Later Collected Poems* are lawless art. *Paterson*, which he says is the pride of locality, is a word-manual for the journeyman poet, and its hard river words will yield much pleasure to the reader. Socrates once said that the misuse of words induces evil in the soul, and this remarkable observation is very close to the problem of the Paterson poem; Williams had a martial passion for the sentence — his phrases have the firing-power of an automatic revolver. Bleak mountain skill, or what we call poetic invention, can slay the spirit. Originality is often a stepmother Muse that gives her breast to the hawk and the mountain, and is the greatest curse in our literature; there is a surfeit of originality in *Paterson*.

Williams was a congealed river-and-rock man who wrote a very remarkable hot book, *In the American Grain*. But our most gifted writers have too much seawater in their heads, and all of them were cold men. Let it be enough here just to mention Thoreau's *Walden* and *A Week on the Concord and Merrimack Rivers*, for the titles of these wonderful volumes are ample proof of their contents. Melville's *Moby-Dick* is an astonishing but inhuman masterpiece. Shale and river books are not wisdom literature. Hawthorne, who had as polar a soul as Thoreau, cried out against his boreal nature. In "The Christmas Banquet" Hawthorne writes that to be cold is the most wretched plague of the heart; yet the debile, sinning husband of Hester Prynne in *The Scarlet Letter* is Chillingworth.

The early Greek thinkers believed that where there was too much moisture there was injustice, saying that man at first was a seagoing shark; correct science or not, this is an unusual truth about people. Take heed, then, of those wild, watery men in literature, and remember that Odysseus is miserable until his hapless water-journey is ended, and that he pines not so much for Penelope as for Ithaca, his swine, sheep, and fruits.

A poet ought to be one, to have a single deity that wills and purposes for his whole nature. We imagine a writer to be both Diogenes and Hercules, blunt speaking and a moral force. Without Hercules' lion's skin and club, philosophy and poetry and science are deceitful, profligate, and will-less. We look in vain for moral volition in *Paterson* and *The Later Poems*, for the rocks that simulate fortitude are inhumanities and the water is death. Heraclitus said that too much moisture is death to the soul. It is true that poets have more unstable water in them than other thinkers; Plutarch is more reliable than Shakespeare. There is no mistaking the riggish vices of such caitiffs as Antony and Cleopatra in Plutarch, but there is enough anarchy in the great English poet to confuse the reader, and these wantons are plumaged peacocks with astonishing Asiatic lusts, which Shakespeare forces us to admire. However, Iago had one nature, reechy Goneril is single, and Timon is of one stuff.

The American poet is double, his character chameleon, and he has double moral hands, unlike the philosopher Charles S. Peirce who wrote out his questions with one hand and answered them with the other. As for Williams, it is impossible to know what his affections or his morals are; he so constantly changes his shape that he is like that ever-changing debtor in the comedy of Epicharmos who refuses to pay his creditor because he says he is no longer the same person who borrowed the money. We cannot be in moral debt to Williams because we do not know what he owes us either in negations or in a straight honest yes. In art, as Dostoevski has written, two plus two equals five, and this provides for the underground nihilism in modern man; but in morals two and two are always four. The distinction between art and ethics cannot be so considerable as to make it almost impossible to know the difference between the false and the true, between Acheron and the tender, growing earth. Either we are to get health from a poet or else all this sick water-verse will drive us mad.

We cannot put upon a poet a creed or religion, but he must have one character or we will have the most dreary pluralistic morals, a moral for every new occasion. The shabbiest cynics at Athens had a few lentil, lupin, and thyme rules by which they lived and were recognized. One finds this hardy fare of customs and morals in Homer and in those philosophical dogs who slept and cohabited in the public porches and were as houseless, unblanketed, and unroofed as the Paterson poem, and one of whom offered the following recipe for his pupils: "Set aside ten minas for a chef, a drachma for the doctor, five talents for a flatterer, a talent for a whore, three obols for a philosopher." It is this kind of receipt that we call style or form in a poet or thinker, and whether it is reckoned good or not, it is clear. We blame man less for a principle we may not agree with, and reject, than for his confusion, which we may not comprehend and accept; confusion is the begetter of the greatest evil in the soul.

It is impossible to know whether Williams is a man-hater or not, for though he employs a people's language, the bare hummocks, the "treeless knoll," and the waterworks in the poems are nomadic nihilism. "The water married to the stone" is not pioneer hardihood but supine pessimism and dingy misanthropy. He is homeless and parentless, begotten by January ravines, and always *outside* among "humped roots," "calcined husks," with "rock, bole and fangs"; his affections, moreover, are so *natured* that he can neither house, kitchen, nor table man or earth. The words "stone" and "rock" appear seventy-eight times, and "falls" nineteen times; besides these, "river" and "stream" occur perhaps even more often than the stones, and "gorge," "ledge," "precipice," and "cataract" are also reiterated. Toward the end of the long poem divided into four parts, Williams gives us a log which tells the amount of shale and red sandstone that are at the various depths of a well. "Fanged-toothed rock," "grasshopper of red basalt," and "gulls upon the ice-strewn river," look at first like force and stoicism — we often mistake what is raw and primitive for innocence and primal strength — but are really cold, wet verse.

It is the letters in *Paterson* that are the sun and the blood, the human cry and the conscience absent in the shale and pickerel-weed. The most rancorous epistles are written by an anonymous woman bitterly chiding this man who has become place, for place can be a liar and devour us. The woman writes that the poet has metamorphosed her faculties into some "impenetrable congealed substance," "rough ice." An Egyptian osier burial basket has more human warmth than those feral, cold nature poems.

To use Platonic language, what is in the world must have its counterpart in universals, that is, horse as a particular of the world must be represented by universal horseness, and a chair must have its ideal chairness. In *Don Quixote* the barber's basin is also the helmet of Mambrino; if the one is not also the other, we have either common matter as it is precisely uttered by Williams, or inhuman abstractions, and one without the other is confusion and madness. Melville writes in *Moby-Dick*, "Be thou in the world, but not of it," which counsels a man to be familiar with Polonius and Hamlet, Christ and Barabbas, and to be able to know one from the other. Williams tells the reader of the *Later Poems* to be reconciled with the world, advice that is likely to beget a charlatan, a busybody, and a liar, and that is what the world has been to every real poet, including Jesus who cries out, "O I have overcome the world!"

Both Thoreau and Williams relish a tawny sentence; *The Concord and Merrimack* and *In the American Grain* are American canonical geography; Williams has submitted to Greenland and to savage territory as much as he dares. He wrote with deep understanding of the pilgrims that came to conquer a vast wilderness continent and were possessed by it. Take the following phrases out of these two authors' volumes and judge whether they belong to Thoreau or to Williams: "eels and a moon," "rock, bole and fangs," "sweet-barked sassafras," "treeless knoll," "pumice-covered," "calcined husks," "file-sharp grass," "flint arrow head," "old swale." Do not think this American literary geology is of trifling value, not to be remembered. Homer also has his catalogues of ships, of names, and of towns, and they are poems. There was a writer of Greek comedies by the name of Mermippus who in 429 B.C. drew up a list of imports which are edible verses, for the mind eats what it perceives, and it must thrive and not sicken upon its food: "Hides and vegetable relish from Cyprus; grains and meat from Italy; pork and cheese from Syracuse; sails and papyrus from Egypt . . ." One cannot feed too long on the bogs of Thoreau or on the ravished gravel and grubby river Paterson; those that fall in love with this wild, malignant beauty will be sorely wounded by it. Thoreau and Williams are frontier minds, with an acute wind-and-bramble logic of the physical ground, but all earth is not suitable habitation for the imagination. I can't talk to rocks and trees, says Socrates.

Look at this poet William Carlos Williams: he is primitive and native, and his roots are in raw forest and violent places; he is word-sick and place-crazy. He admires strength, but for what? Violence! This is the cult of the frontier mind. "The hungry animal underlying all other power." He has succumbed to the frontier ground no less than Crèvecoeur, Fenimore Cooper, Twain, and Parkman. But who wants to read these American anchorites on bleak ravines and desolate scrub-pines just to be more inhuman than one already is by nature? What Shakespeare truth or Jeremiah vision is there in these cankered mists and gulches?

Paterson is a homeless, desperado poem; it's all outdoors. "Hypaethral" is the word Thoreau uses. The Paterson Falls is icy nihilism. The poet longs to leap from the ledge into the fatal ice flood, but he has the minister's wife and a tight-rope walker fall into the February river, and when it is dredged the bodies are found, ice-caked. "Rather the ice than their way." But this is fearful ice-sickness, which is the dread of human touch and being involved with people. That's all there is to those cataracts, the waterworks, and the rapids; he knows it but as animal skin has knowledge. Melville was also a lawless cold writer; he wrote *Mardi* to heat his blood. *In the American Grain* is Williams's one hot book, with tropical Aztec and Florida Indian names, and reptile and alligator sexuality, with "sugar cane from the Canaries," "the oil of walnuts . . . drawn like olive oil," "Chicaca . . . stocked with maize," and "loaves made of pulp of plums." The jasper floor of Montezuma's palace is as asiatic as Menelaus's dwelling. There is a lovely chant to Raleigh where Williams writes, "the true form escapes in the wing, sing O Muse . . . of the pursuit of beauty and the husk that remains . . . sing O Muse." But Williams, understanding the tabu fear of touch of the American returns in *Paterson* and in the *Later Collected Poems* to the "hard, repressive pioneer soil of the mind." The poet desires to be place, "the gap between touch and thing." But can locality judge the heart, the liver, and the affections? Like Melville who succumbed to the Pacific, Williams says goodbye to Montezuma, Joppa, Nineveh, and disappears in the Paterson River. He is just homeless, without parent, or man or woman to be near; a prey of the fiercest elements. There is no creative metamorphosis but brutish submission and the cowering animal feeding upon its own paws.

The writing Ishmael bothered Williams. He had a fine imaginative faculty but distrusted books. He made some observations about Dante, Isaiah, and the Aztecans. Like all pioneers Williams hated the old world, and took his revenge upon the old European culture. He thought that the ancient civilizations could not be seeded here, which is a frontier perversion. Melville turned to Job and Lear, Thoreau to the *Bhagavad-Gita*, and Charles S. Peirce used Duns Scotus. Woe be to him who lets any of his higher faculties remain unexplored, wrote Thoreau.

No people require maxims so much as the American. The reason is obvious: the country is so vast, the people always going somewhere, from Oregon apple valley to boreal New England, that we do not know whether to be temperate orchards or sterile climate. Great cultures come out of small Homeric or Hebraic lands; our bigness has given us such humbug size that we are too big for pity or sorrow or for others. Is a man given a talent to use it for himself alone? What our genius lacks most is being simple. If that is clear a poet won't reject his head, as Williams did, because it will smell, according to the Upanishads, like a raven's nest. He will not, like Williams, take up violence in his arms as a bride.

When a poet has some abiding morals in him he can make whatever images he likes, for it will be clear to him that books are the lilies and birds that are more than raiment and meat.

We must return to *In the American Grain*, the genius of the wild and the savage flower in Williams. He tells us a dark parable, and he was the first to gather up American history as a fabulist. He relates how the discoverers came to plant the old European soul here, and though they killed and subdued everything, it was they who were enslaved by primitive river and mountain. The planters were fierce ice men, Red Eric, Hudson, La Salle, Cartier, De Soto, Raleigh. We think Christian nonresistance archaic Asian wisdom, and do not understand how old in lore was brave Montezuma, who submitted to Cortes and a miserable small band, giving him rubies, gold, emeralds, knowing what has always been Indian knowledge, that the conqueror will be the slave. Even the Aztecan names — Napateca, Caliquen, Paraxcoxi — are ancient volcanic gods which enter us as we kill them.

We are still discoverers, new-world logicians, mistaking the Pharaoh cliffs of New Mexico and Arizona and that Egyptian Nile peninsula, Florida, for the ancient epical civilization. There is a terrible truth in this American fable; every discoverer we have had has been a wild homesteader among the seers of the world. Melville, Thoreau, Parkman, Prescott, and Williams are all river and sea and plateau geniuses, ranging a continent for a house, and all of them outdoors.

NO LOVE AND NO THANKS

MANY PEOPLE ASSUME that one age is not worse than another, and that men are not more rigidly ruled by conscience in one generation than in succeeding ones. We have been witnessing a terrible decline in government, scruples, morals, and education. Who can compare the present men in Washington with Jefferson at Monticello, going about in a soiled dressing gown, and in rubbishy house-slippers, maintaining his residence only because his creditors were kind? What rough frontier Seneca can take the place alongside Andrew Jackson who returned to the Hermitage in Tennessee with ninety dollars in his wallet? God bless a humble, democratic indigence, for it is the parent of probity. We look in vain for a Cicero, a much-maligned Andrew Johnson, or even the terrible bigot of the reconstruction period, Thaddeus Stevens, who at least had character if not wisdom. What we require, as Kierkegaard wrote, is not a new form of government, but another Socrates.

The first thought that comes to mind is that a people who are continually demolishing old landmarks — the white farmhouse, the brownstones —

where native genius and spirit once dwelt, are more prepared for war than for peace. No country has suffered so much from the ruins of war while being at peace as the American. There are Mexican laws forbidding avaricious and predatory realtors from erecting homes or offices or business places that do not conform with the character of the adobe dwellings in Taxco or in Cuernavaca. In Paris what an ease it is to memory, the heart's honeycomb, to see the many memorial plaques to Heine, to Berlioz, to Balzac, or the building where Strindberg once lived. At 137 Waverly Place, Poe composed some of his works. The rather dilapidated structure is occupied by a Mexican restaurant, and there is nothing on the bricks but grim vacancy. "Lo, the past is prophecy," said Herman Melville.

Students learn more reverence, homage, and courtesy from contemplating a house, a room, or a desk used by a Melville, a Whitman, a Poe, than from a congealed, academic reading of the *Iliad*, or "Ligeia." A nation that destroys old landmarks and sacral places eradicates love and learning. Melville went to the Holy Land to weep over the footprints of the Nazarene. Several years ago the English poet Herbert Read sent me a clymene which he had plucked from Agamemnon's tomb. Wisdom is tender remembrance. Ask the living what recollections he has of Anderson, Randolph Bourne, Dreiser, Stieglitz, and you will know whether he himself has not died.

Every time I go by the Brevoort I wonder how soon this building will be the booty of greedy men and the ruin of recollection.* Less than a century ago the Minetta Stream sported through the Brevoort Meadow farms.

It is with hard, grum eyes that I look at the new buildings on the Square. Constructed of gimcrack bricks in which the blood has been killed, these edifices now stand in the place of the red Rhinelander houses and the old Strunsky apartments, the abode of so many painters. Strunsky, a guttural, waddling old man in a shambling suit, reminded one of Marc Chagall's ghetto Jew with a fiddle and long rabbinical coattails. He was more of a tintype rags and bottle picker than a propertied man, and loved a glass of

* This essay was written in 1952 before the old Brevoort was torn down.

Chianti or a Lais of the Village, and was always being duped by his impecunious roomers, who were bizarre wastrels or journeymen authors.

Almost everybody of the arts lived in a Strunsky room at one time or
another. The Strunsky Third Street rooms, shaken by the elevated trains,
faced a garden which divided the scummy Lazaruses of the muses from
the rich tenants who occupied the apartments on the Square. Once, when
I came to Strunsky to rent a room, and told him I could not bear the Third
Avenue El, he said, "Stay a week or two, rent free, and if you don't like it,
leave." I knew a painter, one of the many artistic freebooters who were
Strunsky's tenants. Strunsky, who was either embarrassed about asking
him for the rent or busy drinking a flagon of wine, sent his agent. The
agent, after making his call, lent the painter ten dollars. The artist had
borrowed the money for oils and canvas, and a few frugal meals.

There were many rascals whom Strunsky kept. He walked with slow,
heavy labor; he often could not keep up with some of his tenants, who
broke into unoccupied apartments to avoid him. Three of them, who had
a pair of white mice, picked locks and changed their chambers continually;
when they were cold, like Diagoras the Greek sophist who broke up a
statue of Hercules for firewood, they cast Strunsky's rockers and tables
into the open hearth.

Rents were modest, food reasonable and often good, for this was before
the simple cafe was replaced by the Eighth Street ulcer food stations with
their chromium Greyhound bus fronts. Poetry is scant in a land when the
prices for potatoes, milk, and vegetables are immoral. It is not idle to
report that Euripides' mother was a huckster of herbs and watercress, and
though Aristophanes lampooned Euripides because of his mother's humble occupation, Aristophanes himself was the poet of persimmons and
goat's milk, and some of his best lines are fragrant with mint, anise seeds,
and Minerva's olive.

The Bleecker Street carts, once a pleasure-place for shoppers, painters,
and novelists, are now run by ruffian vendors more thievish than the fish-
mongers of ancient Athens. High prices have made the customers and

storekeepers morose and testy. The erstwhile Penelopes and Helens of Troy on Cornelia and Carmine Streets now have sharp, guillotine faces.

Macdougal Alley, an embalmed showplace, with studios ornamented with nineteenth-century carriage lanterns and a cobbled walk like old Salem, is occupied by wealthy, artistic amateurs. One has to be a millionaire to live there or at Washington Mews. The Mews was once a livery stable, then servants' quarters, and afterwards a refuge for penurious bohemians, but the houses are now chic little manors for handsomely paid ad-copy writers. Sherwood Anderson, who furtively penned *I'm a Fool* when he was supposed to be writing automobile copy in Chicago, lived with the wealthy Emmets at 54 Washington Mews when he was not in Marion, Virginia, or at his nearby house in Troutdale. He was lucky because Burton Emmet, a big advertising man, was his friend. When Anderson was poor and obscure, Emmet asked him how much he wanted for one of his manuscripts, which may have been *Dark Laughter*. Anderson's manuscript was not worth anything and so he joshingly said to Emmet, "Oh, you can have it for five thousand dollars," and the kind Emmet gave it to him. Anderson used the money to start two grassroots newspapers in Marion, one Democratic and the other Republican.

Anderson aped everybody he thought could teach him, for the best writing is the imitation of good prose. Most of our contemporary originals have no masters, or they mimic other bad authors, and that is why their prose is ignorant and brutish. Anderson must have been influenced by Edgar Howe, embittered author of a bleak Kansan novel, *The Story of a Country Town*, which seems to have been a model for *Winesburg, Ohio*. Besides that, Edgar Howe ran an honest provincial paper in Atchison. Howe, known in his prime as the sage of Potato Hill, died as late as 1937, at an old age; he was a seedy, forgotten figure by then. We savagely forget our writers, for we are like the lotus-eaters in Homer, who eat the sleepy poppies in order to annihilate our origins and homeland.

On Eleventh Street the Rhinelander apartments are set back of a midwestern yard glutted with weedy grass and rough-coated geraniums, surrounded by porches and iron galleries that look like those in the creole

31]

latin quarter of New Orleans. Theodore Dreiser occupied a pair of small rooms here where he wrote *An American Tragedy*. Dreiser was no outlandish bohemian; he had little patience with exaggerated or *outré* raiment, long, unbarbered hair, or affected sandals, suits, and ties. He came, like Aristophanes, just before an era of the wildest impudicities. Without shame, there is no courtesan so wanton as the writer.

Dreiser was a hot doubter of God, a Hoosier preoccupied with the Sermon on the Mount, Ecclesiastes, Shakespeare, spiritualism, and Christian Science. He stepped out of the pages of the American novel of the seventies and eighties, Eggleston's *Circuit Rider*, Robert Herrick or Henry B. Fuller's Chicago narratives. He was very much concerned with an American tradition of bitterness in letters; Dreiser wrote pieces on Fuller and Harold Frederic, and another on the intransigent Randolph Bourne, which appeared in the *American Spectator* and which I later reprinted in *Twice a Year*.

There is a great hatred and nether fear of negations in America. It is very perplexing how an intrepid frontier people, who fought a wilderness, floods, tornadoes, and the Rockies, cower before criticism, which is regarded as a malignant tumor in the imagination. We are a most solitary people, and we live, repelled by one another, in the gray, outcast cities of Cain. We are always talking about being together, and yet whatever we invent destroys the family, and makes us wild, touchless beasts feeding on technicolor prairies and rivers.

It was to be expected that Dreiser, who came after bitter Bierce, Hamlin Garland, and Fuller, should have been very much interested in iconoclasm as well as in compromise. His portrait of Harris Merton Lyon, who is De Maupassant, Jr., in *Twelve Men*, is about an acerb nature, a gifted writer who could no longer bear penury and limbo. Harris Merton Lyon is the author of two books, *Sardonics* and *Graphics*, which are no more than epitaphs in our literary graveyard. They were published by William Marion Reedy, who had married the mistress of a house of ill fame in St. Louis, and from whose illicit revenues he was able to print books. Both Stephen

Crane and Marion Reedy married women whom they had met among the tombs of pleasure.

Merton Lyon, like so many of our writers, had had enough of the blood and the tears on the Mount of Olives, and went to that garden of sodomy, Hollywood. Dreiser was a shrewd speculator in human beings, and he weighed his conduct toward each person he knew or met. Merton Lyon, the young, bellicose rebel, bullied him, but Dreiser did not mind, because the amount of talent in the world is as small as the cummin seed. Dreiser had one behavior for the castaway Lazarus of letters and another for art entrepreneurs; an ambitious painter, who thought that art was a Jacob's ladder to mammon rather than to angelic vision, complained that when he called on Dreiser to do a caricature of him which was to be included in a book on famous men, King Dreiser received him while sitting in a regal armchair on a dais.

Many regarded Dreiser as an ugly Thersites, but I was unusually interested in the large, bulky Hoosier whose face was already dented by age, alcohol, and the vanity of vanities. Old Dreiser had a white, wolvish face, and a shaggy underlip on which there was as much ribald, rabelaisian laughter as there was the sorrow of the Preacher in Ecclesiastes. When I first met him I asked why he had written those anti-semitic letters to Hutchins Hapgood, the anarchist, which the *Nation* printed. He said that his publisher, Horace Liveright, a Jew, had cheated him. Could he, I queried, have expected greater honesty from Jay Gould or J. P. Morgan had they published him? It was curious that Dreiser, who had joined the communists, who are supposed to be free of such malevolent miscreeds, should so speak. It was also startling because Dreiser was an ardent admirer of Gustavus Meyer's *History of Great American Fortunes*, in whose volumes none of the big brigands who have slain America is a Jew.

Few of Dreiser's private words regarding the Gospels, or the poet of *Coriolanus* and *Lear* and *Timon of Athens*, for it was Shakespeare as the fabulist of man eating man that concerned him most, got into his books. Then the wisest books are riddles in a poet's tomb, and I think his best books lie with his remains. He must have had great doubts about his works, for I remember how chagrined I felt when I heard he had bowed to Steinbeck.

Once Dreiser asked me whether I could tolerate the novels of James T. Farrell, and I replied, having a stronger stomach at that time for American street-gamin books, that I could. Farrell, and his first wife, Dorothy, were living in a sour Village room, in the gaslight poverty of a Stephen Crane short story. Their fare was tomato juice and dry crackers.

I took a great fancy to the hairy Esau tough from Chicago. He was very belligerent because everybody attacked his books, and he had a gay, assassin's tongue for such quack rebels as Mike Gold, Joe Pass, and Alexander Trachtenberg, who was once the Oriental rug peddler of American Communist literature. When Farrell sold his manuscripts — a great bundle of sacral trash — to the Newberry Library, he also gave them his Chinese laundry ticket as a precious relic of his immortality. I did not mind his illiteracy very much, for I have always had unusual misgivings about American grammar culture; I was, I think, his first, and certainly most ardent advocate. However, Farrell soon became a sly mammon radical, desiring to be the successful and well-established heretic with an apartment at Beekman Place. Farrell's books came fast. The interval of time between novels, or what Melville called the grass-growing silences between one creation and another, was not for Farrell. Soon he was a well-known bad writer. When he was shaken by poverty, doubt, and obscurity I had come to him after reading *Gas-House McGinty,* and said I did not wish to attack the book, and add to his hardships, but that I could not praise it either, and so would not review it for the *Nation.*

I don't know whether people compromise or just fathom their own natures. A writer does not have to be a great reader, but what he does read should be good and honest, and as wise as dust can be. I think a poet could say all that he had to with two or three books, the Bible, Shakespeare, and William Blake, provided he is a man of great feeling, and that is the only difference between a gross and lymphatic man and an artist. Farrell, coming from a poor Catholic Irish-American family, was a scatological atheist himself, with no real knowledge of the Bible or of any other masterpiece.

36 Grove Street, where I lived in 1933, was a rendezvous for Farrell, Waldo Frank, John Herrmann, Norbert Guterman, Joshua Kunitz, Sol Funaroff, Nathan Asch, Josephine Herbst, and many others. Hortense Alden, the ingenue of *Grand Hotel*, and a frequent visitor at 36 Grove, told me that she loathed Farrell's works; but later, after she married him and they held soirees at their place on Lexington Avenue, she kept a notebook and wrote down every platitude that came out of the mouth of the author of *Studs Lonigan*. Let those who fear failure flee in horror from that squalid Nemesis called Success. The Farrell story is a dirty fable, all about money and stupidity. "The reason that dullness is so much farther advanced than genius," said Samuel Butler, "is that it is so much better organized."

What distressed me very much was the utter lack of self-detachment in these people. Ambition is a Dead Sea fruit, and the greatest peril to the soul is that one is likely to get precisely what he is seeking. There was a narcissism in these novelists that impelled them to write the same books all their lives. More American writers have been slain by success than by any other affliction. Though oblivion is a very hard taskmaster, I could never be a well-to-do votary of helicon. The literary Narcissus seldom troubles to look at another man. He has a dead, ravine heart, and as he sees no one but his own books or words or reflections, he does not even believe that other people exist. We rarely see anybody any longer; little wonder that Peguy felt that we now live in a peopleless world. There was Paul Rosenfeld, who, after reading a book of mine on American literature, *Can These Bones Live*, asked Kenneth Patchen whether he could not arrange to meet me, although I had known him for thirteen years.

The Marxists and the Narcissists gave us the false vineyards of Pisgah; these were the foxes that spoiled our vines. There is the little story of the deceit of Scholem Asch. Nathan Asch once asked me whether I would give his father, Scholem, a dinner as he was a stranger just coming to America from Nice. About twenty-five writers came, including Waldo Frank, John Herrmann, author of *What Happened*, which had been published in Paris in the heyday of the expatriates, his wife Josephine Herbst, who had a fine, peasant figure and a straight, robustious way of expressing her beliefs. She is the author of that tender volume on Bartram, *New Green World*, and the remarkable portrait of Nathanael West, "Hunter of Doves." There were Mike Gold, who lived downstairs and who picked his nose because, I imagine, it made him feel closer to the lower classes, and Norbert Guterman. Sometime after dinner Scholem Asch approached me and said, with thick, deliberate words, that his son, Nathan, had told him I was a very gifted writer, and that if I would give him my books and inscribe them to him, he would get them translated into six different European languages. I thanked him and gave him three of my novels. Scholem Asch returned to Nice, and I never heard from him. Nine months later I told Nathan Asch what had occurred and he said, "Whenever father wants the books of authors for nothing he always tells them that he will get their books translated into six different languages."

There was Edmund Wilson, a cultivated young critic, who I thought would become a Taine, or a Montesquieu, or a Lessing. His red hair was thinly scrawled on his pate; he had a pugnacious mouth and a handsome nose. What he lacked was not pertinacity, or the enthusiasm for work, but an inward nature; it has always taken him twenty years to make a right judgment about a bad book. He continues, however, to make the same mistakes about the same imbecilic books, but written by different authors. Edmund Wilson has the literary stomach of an alligator who can eat everything — sticks, stones, and the grossest fiction; he can swallow a seven-hundred-page novel whole, without chewing or tasting it though it contains great lumps of graveled clichés. Once, walking with him to Grand Central Station, I thanked him profusely for comparing me with Huysmans, and he replied that he had just done that to help the sales of the novel. I went away feeling sad and impoverished.

Kenneth Fearing, a very neglected poet of little tombstone ironies on America, never troubled to thank Sol Funaroff and me for bringing out his verse. Funaroff, a radical poet, and one whose spirit was not staled by selfishness, spent days at the printers for Fearing's book, while I went to various editors and acquaintances to raise the money. I wrote a foreword to it and got Archibald MacLeish, Joshua Kunitz, and Farrell to speak at an evening given at a lawyer's house on Twelfth Street. The book sold and was well received, and Fearing got a Guggenheim award. Now, as the author of *The Big Clock*, he is like Frank and Farrell and others of the clock tribe of the fast word.

Ford Madox Ford's one recipe for the spirit in travail was work, and more work, and though most of the authors were always busy either beginning or finishing a bad novel, Ford did not mean laboring to be a cash register artist. In the *Bhagavad-Gita* it is said: "He who works without attachment, resigning his actions to Brahma, is untainted by sin, as a lotus-leaf by water." I have known the humbug lowly Lazaruses of verse. They were meek when they had to eat their piece of limbo alone in a shabby Village room, but were given to the most unendurable pompous braying as soon as they had any recognition.

Kenneth Patchen used to visit me later at 2 Grove Street. He came at first to bring his poems, and afterward to hear me reject them. He was meeker than the Galilean before Herod. Each time I had to send him away, telling him quite sorrowfully that he ought to read more and write less. A few years afterwards he and his Finnish wife paid me a visit. When she permitted him to talk he assailed Shakespeare. This was at the time when the Soviets had attacked Finland. I was so vexed with her interruptions that, though I was very anti-Soviet, I hoped that the Russians would invade Finland all over again. Once Dostoevski said that someone had given him the basest affront by insulting Christ. I regard Shakespeare as the Christ of poetry.

One day at An American Place, Stieglitz, who could not stomach the peacock in Waldo Frank, told me he had received the following letter from a lady in Truro, where Frank spent his summers as a mammon cenobite of vision. The woman had written: "My dear Mr. Stieglitz, I have told Waldo that he is an admixture of Aeschylus, Goethe, Spinoza and Beethoven, and still he is very disconsolate. You who are wise, tell me, please, what I should do for Waldo?" Stieglitz replied: "My dear lady, do precisely what you have been doing." Stieglitz had done a charming photograph of

Waldo Frank, a young, forty-year-old cherub, eating an apple. The apple is the fruit of sex, and Frank is always writing about sex as though no one else had ever eaten the apple.

I think the main fault with these men is that they lacked self-knowledge. How many people have the courage to know even a tithe of themselves? They were, at best, logicians of the heart, and pray, what can reason tell us of feeling? Pascal said: Reason invariably surrenders to feeling. There is no animal that is so unreasonable as man.

These Bohemian word-mongers primped their vanity more than women do. They were such loud crowing art roosters. What has a writer to be bombastic about? Whatever good a man may write is the consequence of accident, luck, or surprise, and nobody is more startled than an honest writer when he makes a good phrase or says something truthful. Writing well is as much of a miracle as a wise perception, and the person least responsible for this is the author himself.

The worst canker is jealousy. Somebody praised Faulkner to Hemingway who, after reading Faulkner's novels, said, "I don't have to worry about Faulkner." I remember with anguish the first time I saw a young, unknown, and unpublished poet, Horace Gregory. He was sorely crippled, and it was a pain to watch him twitch his elbows as he attempted to hold and light a cigarette. Marya Zaturenska, from New York's East Side, and wife of Horace, was so skinny that she seemed partly paralytic. She used to sweep dust out of one corner and into another mumbling to herself and to me that she was a better poet than Horace. She showed me a manuscript of poems which I said she should throw away, for which she some time later received a Pulitzer award. What publishers require are not shrewd readers, but clairvoyants whose opinion on trash should be of immense value to them. I remember advising Putnam's in London not to bring out *The Conscience of Zeno* by the friend of Joyce. The book was enormously popular abroad and here.

I have always hated any kind of pretense in people, and have no use at all for busy poets. The devotees of verse are idlers, like Socrates who took time to teach Aspasia, the famous courtesan and mistress of Pericles, the arts of love. Ovid must have been that sort of drone, for he wrote a book about amours.

At that time I wrote a long letter to T. S. Eliot, urging him, as guilefully as I could, to publish Gregory's *Chelsea Rooming House*. Having had no word from him in several months, I sent him a strong rebuke. After I mailed the letter, I received a reply from Eliot, telling me that he was ready to bring out Gregory's poems. Sick with anguish over what I had done, I crawled into a subway, sitting in that iron season of hell until I arrived at the Church Street post office. I showed the postal superintendent my credentials, and asked him whether there was the slightest chance of re-covering the letter I had written. He asked a clerk to look through the foreign-mail bags, and the letter was returned to me.

Gregory was as bent and twisted as Randolph Bourne, the brave hunch-back who lived in the Village in 1918 and wrote *Untimely Papers*. Gregory was a supple reader, and had a yellow, wrinkled laugh that was not un-pleasant to those who knew him. Most people are jealous of the favors of Aphrodite, but Gregory and Marya had not the spartan courage to allow that another person could write a good book. Gregory once told me with ecstasy that his father, a wealthy Milwaukee confectioner, had ruined Hart Crane's father, who was a big businessman in sweetmeats in Cleveland.

The Gregorys gave many parties at which one met an outlandish assort-ment of people: Roslyn Hightower, former wife of Melvyn Douglas, the motion picture star, and Muñoz-Marin, whose father was a Puerto Rican revolutionary hero. Marin wrote for *Smart Set* and chased American women. He is now governor of Puerto Rico, but then had the most gaudy passion for Gladys Oaks, formerly the wife of Bill Gropper, the cartoonist. Joe Gould often came to visit or for food or to take care of their little four-year-old girl, Joanna, who had rude, electric health. She used to know what guest was working on a novel or a biography or verse, and would say to a visitor, "Are you going to dedicate your book to my Daddy?"

Joe Gould lived at the Mills Flophouse on Bleecker Street, where he wrote the annals of our century in a hundred public school composition books. I had given a small portion of it to Richard Johns, publisher of

Pagany, who printed it. Richard Johns himself was a gallant man, supported by a father who owned two burlesque houses on Scollay Square in Boston. Gould was the American Lazarus par excellence; he wore the scummiest clothes, and when he was able to eat, he sat for hours in Stewart's cafeteria, brushing mustard on dry white bread. Until he died he trudged the Village streets in a potter's field suit, with his long, weedy beard like a dead mummy's growing hair. He would go to the door of old acquaintances or friends, like E. E. Cummings, who gave him fifty cents or a dollar. His memory was not incisive toward the end, and sometimes people at whose door he stood would tell him that he had been there the day before, but ask him to return when his allowance was due him. A graduate of Harvard, and of old New England stock, he had a beaky-nosed wit, and no one gave a Village party without asking him to come. One of his many epigrams was, "Sometimes I awaken, and have the grand delusion that I am Joe Gould."

Almost anything was possible at the Gregory place: the locks were no good, doorknobs rolled down the steps; if one drew the shade, it fell, or when one went to the bathroom, he could not get out. On Saturday nights there was tumult. A hulking Icelander, who frequently came there, ran up and down the stairs one Saturday evening, pursuing a woman with an ice-pick, which may be the national tool of that country. On this occasion a young American matron, married to a Japanese, was being pressed by an ardent suitor; finally she threw up her hands, exclaiming, "Don't touch me, I'm the wife of the author of *The House with the Grass Roof*!"

Samuel Putnam, who had a deep mark on his forehead like the crucifix in Ahab's face, and who translated *Don Quixote*, was often there. Maxwell Bodenheim and Minna his wife were also frequenters of the Gregorys. At this time, unable to make money out of his verse, Bodenheim had devised a scheme for writing salable novels for telephone operators, typists, and factory girls. One of these he called *Replenishing Jessica*, which must have been read by lonely, avid men, and another he titled *Naked on Roller Skates*, which was the cause of great torment to the Bodenheims' son, who was then at Ethical Culture School. Every day after school let out, the boys and girls ran up to the Bodenheim boy, and crossing one finger over another to signify shame, screamed, "Naked on roller skates!"

The radical Bohemian was very gregarious, and when not at the *New Masses* or at some bazaar or dancing at Webster Hall, was seen wandering alone in the Village streets like some hurt mind in the fields of asphodels. Despite much babbling about collectivism and the embarrassing use of the word "comrade," he showed a general apathy toward others, and one saw little in this loveless, inert mass-man to make one conceive of him as an utopian. The Marxists, of course, had the greatest scorn for words like utopian, ethics, and love, and Stieglitz himself, always an anti-communist, used to say that love and justice were mere words; it may be true, but those who utter the words often enough are likely to believe in them so fervently as to be loving and kind.

Joshua Kunitz was one of these lonely radical Lucifers who was weary from going to and fro in the earth and from walking up and down in it. I came to know him intimately after he had read a manuscript of his to me and through a *New Masses* kleptomaniac who had murmured low words into the bloodstreams of several authors whose genius he said he was going to make known in a book he was preparing. The kleptomaniac was a very agile taker, and he used to steal volumes from the workers' bookstore, and give them to me with the most plenteous inscriptions to my afflatus, and then rob me of them. He was also studying Mike Gold's genius, and succeeded in depriving him of many letters from Gide, Aragon, Malraux, and Romain Rolland. He told Kunitz about his uncle who he said had served in the Russian Duma, and also of his visit with Trotsky who was in exile at Prinkipio, a Turkish isle. Finally, he made some intricate remarks about the summers in Moscow, after which Kunitz, who had been there, told him he was a liar.

The kleptomaniac had a sly, prehensile nose the shape of a piccolo. After Mike Gold, Kunitz, and me, he paid homage to Waldo Frank. I had warned Frank but he told me I was pessimistic and should devote my mind to the good rather than to the evil in the world. I thought about Sir Thomas Browne's darksome line, that man is noble and splendid in his ashes.

Waldo entertained the kleptomaniac, who took his postage stamp collection, his literary letters from European sages, and his wife, for later the kleptomaniac wrote a book which he dedicated to his mother, father, and to Alma, which was the name of Frank's wife.

For some reason which will always be inscrutable to me, Frank introduced the kleptomaniac to Stieglitz. The kleptomaniac won the confidence of the elder, suspicious Stieglitz, who could sell an O'Keeffe or a Marin to a prospective but lukewarm buyer for five thousand dollars, but was not clever enough to prevent this young cutpurse Autolycus from removing some twenty paintings from An American Place. He promptly sold the Hartleys, O'Keeffes, and Marin watercolors for a hundred dollars or so to members of the Group Theater, including Harold Clurman, Stella Adler, and John Garfield. Though he was a kleptomaniac, he was an aesthetic one, for he never took anything from people who were not recognized artists. Besides, like Thoreau, who said he was too high-born to be propertied, he only disposed of the imponderables of this world, and, at least, he gave them to others at proletarian prices, which horrified Stieglitz.

Kunitz had written a book on Samarkand, that Middle Eastern feudal Asia which the Soviets rule. I thought it an extremely interesting manuscript, which none of the *New Masses* intelligentsia cared for or had ever taken the trouble to read. Kunitz was not word or book trade for the communists. They were only interested in proletarian literature that would sell.

Once after Kunitz had returned from Moscow and walked into the *New Masses* office, no one even greeted him. Depressed, he retired to his cubicle for the day, and in the waning afternoon, the editors called him, and said they had decided to give a party in his honor. A broad smile covered his tartar face, and, humbled by his harsh judgments of these Marxist and Leninist brothers, he thanked them. They asked him about his book on Samarkand which I had praised to Harry Block at Covici and when it would be published. The *New Masses* editors then told Kunitz that they thought a party for him would make money for the movement, and that it would be a fine Stalinist gesture if he would dedicate the book to Angelo Herndon, a southern Negro imprisoned for strike activities, and whom

Kunitz had never met. Kunitz, bewildered because the affair had little or nothing to do with him as a person, docilely obeyed.

One afternoon when Kunitz and I were walking together, he told me that he had made all sorts of acknowledgments to various *New Masses* editors in the book, which he titled *Dawn over Samarkand,* and then in some confusion said, "You were responsible for getting the book published, and I forgot to mention your name. Tell me what to write?" Of course, I would hardly tell him what to write about me in his book. It was typical of that time and now, which is an era of no love and no thanks. Still, Joshua Kunitz was the only Marxist I have ever known who was a human being.

Many handsome sylphs and Venuses from Richmond, Virginia, or from Davenport, Iowa, came to New York to wed or have gamey liaisons with famous Greenwich Village artists. Instead of a Dreiser, or an Anderson, or a Merton Lyon, or a Stephen Crane, they fell in love with cafeteria D. H. Lawrences, or with Louis Bonaparte Vandykes, or with Village Gauguins or Van Goghs in denims and sandals. There was one fine cabinet-maker who had very deft hands in sculpting wood or making a chair or trestle table, and poor ones for oils, but he wanted most to be known as a painter. He met a robust Kansan girl, delightfully naive if foolish, who each morning as she left his studio door, would turn back, and in a high, aqueous voice, cry out, "Create! Create!" Poor thing, I guess she was not adequate for his own artistic defeats and limits, for later he married the widow of William Ellery Leonard, poet and Madison, Wisconsin, professor, who was the sex rebel of the campus, and had such a fear of open spaces. Ellery Leonard, a charming nature, who had translated Lucretius, received a letter from the Viking Press, asking him to commend Richard Aldington's anthology of verse which did not include a single poem of his. It was one of the last knives pressed into his heart; Aldington showed me the pitiable letter he had received from Leonard.

We have become a solitary people because we do so little for others any more. Hamlin Garland tells us that the middle-border pioneer would supply a family of strangers with cows, a horse, corn, butter, if they would settle next to him. Machines have drearily separated us, and people have made a cult of solitude as though it was not the result of baleful industrial inhumanities, but was a vapory good and ideal to be labored for. The ruin of the human heart is self-interest, which the American merchant calls self-service. We have become a self-service populace, and all our specious comforts — the automatic elevator, the escalator, the cafeteria — are depriving us of volition and moral and physical energy. The machine has had a pernicious effect upon virtue, pity, and love, and young men used to machines which induce inertia, and fear, are near impotents. The auto, which means self, is a mechanical pastime, like movies and television; it has broken America as a land for a communal populace. Folk dances, riverbank picnics, walking tours have been replaced by the movie theater in which people, almost impermeably separated from one another, sit together in a vast hole of darkness. This folly of novelties is also an English and French malady, and the Citroen or the Austin are puerile, mechanical playthings for people who crawl in and out of them like embryos. An Austin car is like some of the funny, rolling-auto poems by E. E. Cummings, unreflective and infantile. Unless we return to the old handicrafts, to the wheat, stable, and horse village, to poems, houses, bricks, and tables, which are manual, we will become a nation of killers, for if people do not employ their hands in making what is good, or gentle, or noble, they will be criminals. Malherbe once said, "I have always held my service such a despicable offering that to whatever altar I bring it, it is with a heart ashamed and a trembling hand."

ROBERT McALMON: A MEMOIR

I FIRST HAD THE GOOD LUCK to exchange words with Robert McAlmon in Paris at the Coupole. He was a tubercular bantam with sharp, querulous hair and a thin, exasperated mouth. Everything about him was scant except his prodigal heart and his vocabulary of four-letter words. He was the most obscene man I had ever met. Like every expatriate he had a furtive, underground passion for America, which he would pause to anathematize while mentioning such writers as William Carlos Williams, Lautréamont, or George Antheil. He was the epitome of the self-appointed exile who hated the antiseptic, epicene American town and took the greatest yea-saying joy in depicting it.

McAlmon had been an artist's model in Greenwich Village earning fifty cents an hour when he worked. One day while he was posing a woman approached him and asked him to marry her. She was the daughter of a fantastically wealthy perfume manufacturer in England. The woman told him to think it over for a day or two and that if he were willing she would take him to Paris and furnish him with all the money he required.

The wedlock was a mock one and probably led McAlmon to aberrations and excesses that he would not have indulged in otherwise. Perhaps he found this also a way to flee from those females resembling Scylla, who, Ovid said, had dogs beneath her stomach. When a man is unable to drop his strength into a woman his attitude toward the universe is warped. Buffon remarked that our organs suffer far more from weariness from the longings to which they are subject than from actual physical indulgence. Little wonder that one of the greatest complaints in America is fatigue.

Robert McAlmon was a defiant rake-hell of literature; he went to Paris and later to Barcelona to inveigh against America without restraint. He seemed to lack the full liberty he prized so much unless he could employ the most loathsome words. The money he spent to help and to print the works of unknown authors dropped through his sieve-like pockets just as easily as the gargantuan obscenities fell out of his mouth. A nihilist, he believed that no one could enter the kingdom of letters unless he detested virtue. The expatriate, disciple of Lautréamont's *Maldoror*, canonized evil.

McAlmon had an incisive, malevolent intellect. He published Contact Editions, bringing out the poems and the hectic abscessed ecstasies of a host of fallen angels of genius, including Joyce, Pound, Gertrude Stein, Emanuel Carnevali, John Herrmann, and himself. His own book, *The Distinguished Air*, is done in a clear, brutal prose style; it is absolutely pornographic and positively serious.

Aside from telling me of his admiration for Marianne Moore and that though he thought Joyce and Pound had talent he did not believe that they possessed very efficient minds, I recollect no word of his except "fart." He understood the boundaries of others, but not his own.

We are as small as we imagine we are; a charlatan has a wilder and more rugged terrain than a philister. McAlmon was a chivalric failure, but many of those whose works he published when nobody else would lacked his waspish and unflinching integrity. Whatever were the great faults of McAlmon's novels like *A Hasty Bunch*, his poem on North America, or *The Distinguished Air*, you will not look in vain for that rare ore in human character, honesty, which is lacking in the volumes prattled about in the public whorehouse directory of literature, American newspaper book columns. True, I never read with great interest his *Being Geniuses Together*, which contains a great deal of gossip about Pound, Hartley, Joyce, Marianne Moore, and others. But then I don't have much of a palate for Pepys's or for Evelyn's diary, which may be a fatuous declaration. The real point is that we require strong characters far more than another verse by a well-known nonentity.

Robert McAlmon and John Herrmann, one of whose novels he printed, had bizarre and hapless fates. Years later, and out of pocket, John Herrmann peddled venetian blinds for Mark Antonio in New Orleans, Robert McAlmon sold trusses in El Paso, Texas. Is anything accidental? What an odd and bawdy occupation for a magnificent and lewd nature.

I saw McAlmon again in 1951 when I lived on Washington Square. Josephine Herbst, a gallant of the literati, gave him my telephone number. He called and asked me to come right over to the Albert Hotel, which had once been the elysium of penurious artists and writers. He was drunk, intellectually brisk, and wanted me to assist him in persuading somebody to publish *Being Geniuses Together*. Warburg in London had brought out the book there. I was eager to be useful to him since I owe every talented heart a moiety of my own good luck. Had I the alchemist's stone I would have turned all his rage, bile, and truthful bitterness into gold. But I was helpless; no one was interested in this homeless soul. He had burnt up everybody in the flames of his Ilium, for he thought that anybody who was successful in anything at all was an odious bourgeois.

He had insulted everyone; but then so had the Dadaists who, as well as he, had resolved to be outrageous. We tolerate so many mediocrities but cannot forgive an unusual man. One should save one's stones for the mercenaries of letters, and not cast them at a broken Ishmael of truth.

Then McAlmon became ill and repaired to a scrawny garbage settlement, Desert Hot Springs, the back alley of Palm Springs, where he owned a small stucco duplex. He lived in one part and rented out the other half for forty dollars a month, on which he managed by eating the lean fare of a Greek Cynic or an acolyte of Plotinus. He spent most of this pittance on gallons of bad wine and whiskey. My wife Rlene one day looked into his icebox and saw nothing there but lentils, which reminds one how Diogenes washed leeks in the stream for his supper.

Dying of tuberculosis and alcohol, he had no companions except arthritic she-slovens, consumptive plumbers, and a female real-estate agent with a bone and joint disease who had come there for the mineral baths. He was obscene to the end and so emaciated toward the last months of his life that he made profane remarks about his shrunken genitals. We used to visit him about once every month, for he was utterly forsaken by all the authors who had been obscure and unwanted before they appeared in Contact Editions. It was impossible to raise any interest in him because he was not considered a literary commodity. How many men I have known who buried the poems and novels of their friends because they were not regarded as valuable pieces of merchandise by the literary tradesmen! Of course, McAlmon was already a legend but he had not died, which he was soon to do to accommodate those who neglect the living whose works they immediately embalm when they are dead.

Even in those days of Gehenna for him, he was always intelligent, and he worked when he was not drunk, because we burn in ice when we do not toil.

Alas, I too fell out with him, and I think it is a bad part of my own character that I did not allow him the imperial privilege of a despised and gifted man, the ecstasy of insulting me. One evening after much wine, he belittled work of mine which he had previously admired. How easy it is to be perfidious, since we are Christ and Judas together. Cudgeling my head to see how I could do something for him, I thought of setting up a private press and bringing out *The Distinguished Air*, and even the sequel to *Being Geniuses Together*. I was reading the manuscript in his duplex in the desert while this scant man of bones sat in a rocker looking as though he might quit his clothes altogether. I suggested that I take the sequel back to Santa Monica to finish reading it, but he appeared reluctant and suspicious. Very choleric myself when deeply aroused, I spoke harshly to him. It is easy to say that had I known he was close to the grave I would have

[48

been quiet about this and just let it be. Could tears now make some amends to his ashes, I would water his burial site.

What cause had he to trust anybody: and who but a knave or a coney-catcher can tell another man, "have confidence in me"? We wound everybody, and only cry out when our own flesh is scathed, or even when it is only slightly scratched. He was undeniably brave; how many with his opulent past in Paris, living as he did as a patron of letters, could endure those days in a gross desert town? Maybe his works are apples of the Dead Sea, but such fruit is a marvel also. What was the greatest miracle of energy in him was that in spite of every hindrance, he kept on writing, though not a soul cared: but then we write for nobody, live for nobody, and die for nobody.

We had some genial moments together, either when he read some of the later poems of H.D. aloud to us, or when we gabbled about the old vaudeville songs; on one occasion he picked up a stick and a bowler to represent a music-hall performer and proceeded to do a song and dance as it was performed on the stage long before the cinema deadened all human entertainment and natural recreations.

Well into his sixtieth year he still looked pubescent; there was enough gray in his hair to give him the appearance of a sea-foamed Triton in failing health. He had the fewest books that he valued, but that did not prevent him from taking from his impoverished shelves a rare edition of Lautréamont's *Maldoror*, or one of his own books, which curiously enough was very expensive, and presenting it to me. He would have given me *The Distinguished Air* had he two copies of it, and that book was sold for $20.00 in Paris at Titus's bookshop on the rue du Lambre in 1928.

Robert McAlmon was one of the most generous and absolutely natural human beings I have ever known. Only one real fault did I ever detect in him; he thought, alas, he could make money out of his books. We can drink our cup of chagrin mounted on Rozinante or on our way to Calvary, but not for lucre. St. Theresa has said: "Let me, O Lord, be most ungrateful to the world." Is not the world another word for success, mammon, and renown? McAlmon wanted that ignominy which drains and cheapens the spirit, fame; he who had spent his whole life being infamous. He was weary of the underground reputation he had had abroad, and now that he is in the earth, someone will do a study of this remarkable American nihilist, because only a fool will fail to recognize that beneath the crust of insolence was a well-spring of tenderness.

Written in 1961, Majorca, Spain

THE EXPATRIATES: A MEMOIR

THE EXPATRIATE AMERICAN was a heroic Thersites who had come to Paris to be obscene. He detested beauty, a good prose style, sense, health, and learning, and suffered as much from happiness as he did from boredom. He fled from America because he hated middle-class virtue, nice principles, and success. Nothing in our times has become so unattractive as virtue. I would rather take hellebore than spend a conversation with a good, little man.

Nature makes us miserable in everything we do, and the American author in Europe felt doomed because he had so little preparation for his task. He abhorred the nineteenth-century businessmen of Parnassus — Whittier, Longfellow, Bryant — just as Baudelaire loathed such sluts as de Musset and Béranger. But the exile had less knowledge of his own celestial trade than the juvenile Chatterton. When one does not know how to employ his will without aborting his nature, he has no beginning, no middle nor end to his life. None of the exiles ever ripened, and all of their books were the same.

51]

I spent some time in Paris at the cafes eating the lonely, pariah bread of the expatriate until I became so weary of the Dôme and the Coupole I went to Roquebrune, a small hamlet about fifteen minutes by tram from Monte Carlo, to meet Ethel Moorehead. She had a four-room villa there overlooking the Mediterranean. *This Quarter*, a very spirited small magazine, formerly published in Milan by her and Ernest Walsh, was now solely in her hands.

Ethel Moorehead, who was born in Ireland, had been a dogmatic feminist in England. She had participated in many noisy demonstrations in the streets of London, going to countless meetings of militant suffragettes who, when the word *man* was mentioned, rose like a chorus of furies and shouted, "Shame!" She had a bony, economic body, efficient and direct rather than feminine, and a prominent, waspish nose one might have seen painted on a temple wall at Gaza.

She read what I had brought her at once, and accepted a shoal of free verse, a short story, "The Dream Life of Mary Moody," and an essay on aesthetics titled "Ariel in Caliban." However, she insisted that I ask Eugene Jolas and Eliot Paul of *Transition* to return "The Vaudeville Actor," a story they had already accepted; she wished to be the first one to publish my work. I also had about ten pages of an amorphous tale, and after reading it she said: "Why don't you write a novel?" I had not thought of it then, but as we do not know what we are doing anyway, I decided to begin it. This, too, appeared in *This Quarter* number four as "The Beginnings and Continuations of Lorry Gilchrist," and came out later in a limited edition in London with the title *Bottom Dogs*.

A woman who tells the truth is a man; but in spite of the odor of copperas Ethel Moorehead gave off, she was as amorous as a sparrow. When she met Ernest Walsh, an unpublished versifier, she suggested that together they could start a magazine. Though she was a good many years older than Walsh, they had a liaison which would have tempted any libertine. She allowed him all the freedom to which virilia is entitled.

Nearly all the writers abroad were valetudinaries; a poet in good health is a nuisance. Ernest Walsh had fallen in a Texas airfield in the First World

War, and his lungs were so badly damaged that he could not live for a day without injections. He was starving at the Ritz Hotel in Paris where he had a room filled with six wardrobe trunks. This reminds me of Leonid Andreyev who, when he did not have a penny for soup or potatoes, opened the door to his clothes closet and gaped with stupefaction at three new tuxedos which were hanging there.

Walsh anathematized the venal literati, for money is far more obscene than pornography; though Hemingway's first short story was printed in *This Quarter*, Walsh distrusted this vulgar dollar scribbler.

Walsh had the bravado of a buccaneer; he was defiantly honest. I have always admired the strong assault against the common enemy of literature, the book tradesmen. My own credo has invariably been: "attaquez, attaquez, attaquez." Pound himself in his early days, just after he had written *Personae* and *Lustra* which many of us had so deeply trusted, said: "Name your foe; otherwise, he will declare that your philippic is about somebody else."

Walsh did not belong to the school of ordure, nor was he a romantic scatologist like Pound. He was writing Chaucerian verse in the American idiom when Kay Boyle arrived and, in the rhodomontade of the period, told Walsh that she loved his poetry and that they ought to leave for the mountains at once. She too was straight, flat, and Irish, and had the virile nose of a Babylonian Astarte. Ethel Moorehead provided them with some money, and shortly thereafter Ernest Walsh finally succumbed to the consumption that had eaten at him for so long. When I became acquainted with Ethel Moorehead, however, Walsh had been dead for a brace of years.

She had had trouble with Ezra Pound; having asked him to contribute to *This Quarter*, he had sent her a small poem; after it appeared he demanded $375.00 for it. It was an exorbitant request. She not only paid contributors but also helped to support Emanuel Carnevali who was then dying in Bazzano. She and Walsh had dedicated one issue of *This Quarter* to Ezra Pound, but when Ernest Walsh died and she asked Pound to write something about him, Pound refused. In the next issue of the magazine,

Ethel Moorehead wrote a denunciation of Pound and announced: "I take back the dedication to Ezra Pound." This became the *scandale* of the Dôme, Coupole, and Select cafes.

Following the tradition of Ambrose Bierce who vanished in Mexico, Ethel Moorehead too has disappeared. Like Walsh, Carnevali, McAlmon, and John Herrmann, she was a guerilla fighter of letters, and when she thought she had finished what she had set out to do, she dropped from sight, just as Carnevali, McAlmon, and John Herrmann had done. *This Quarter* afterwards passed into the hands of Edward Titus, husband of Helena Rubinstein, the face-cream millionairess.

John Herrmann too had fled from a laodicean America which, he felt, had deprived him of the force to have powerful experiences. He had a long, thewy frame and handsome face. A conspicuous young writer, he won a couple of prizes for short stories. Then he wrote a novel, *What Happened*, which was brought out by McAlmon in Contact Editions. I had read it long before I met this marvelous erring nature. The volume is done in the American idiom. With the rarest exceptions these tales are as barren and void of timber for fire as the wild region about Lake Titicaca.

John Herrmann acted his tragic fate in comic socks and like McAlmon had a strong bent for the ludicrous. In New Orleans he had had a liaison with a little debauchee whose womb had been recommended by her votaries. When she had a child, Herrmann gave cigars to his friends, but when they congratulated him, he said that he was not the father because he was impotent. How like Rozanov, the author of *Solitario*, who confessed that by the time five virgins offered themselves to him he was unable to lie with them.

Herrmann, no less than McAlmon, was afflicted with boyism and alcohol. Alcohol is perhaps more of an antaphrodisiac than the Pythagorean lettuce, and besides he had worn out his secret parts and his will. He always had what Stendhal regarded as one of the most enviable of all human traits, amiability. He was a four-letter-word artist, but it was profanity rather than malice that flowed from his mouth.

In revolt against America and the watercloset cult of sanitation where nobody was supposed to defecate or smell either good or bad, Herrmann became an epicure of dirt. He did not know how to use his life or his talent. Like most of these cafe Dada boys, he surreptitiously worshiped the agrarian states and pined for the western pinto ponies and the red barns of the old bucolic America, the Ohio and Indiana of Anderson and Dreiser.

Another of these militant waifs was Emanuel Carnevali. He wrote *A Hurried Man*, which was also brought out by McAlmon. When he was fifteen he had left Genoa and gone to Chicago. By the time he reached his nineteenth year he had won the admiration of Sherwood Anderson. Carnevali had no other ability than his genius, so he became a beggar. The only way the urchins of the arts have of keeping money circulating is to borrow it from one another. Money in Bohemia is never idle, which is utopian economics. Unfortunately, the human heart is more often dead than quick, and Sherwood Anderson would not show his face at the door when Carnevali presented himself because he was afraid Carnevali had come to beg.

Dorothy Dudley Harvey, in a compassionate introduction to *A Hurried Man*, told how Carnevali had plucked garbage out of a can in Washington Square, and then, weeping, threw it away. In New York Joel Elias Spingarn employed him as a secretary, but Carnevali decided that the books in that gentleman's library which he did not care for ought to be sold — which he did. Carnevali was defecating on the bourgeois. Spingarn was a very charitable person who had written a learned book, *Literary Criticism in the Renaissance*, but it was like a celebrated baroque church — containing everything that art and tradition can bestow on a building except suffering.

Carnevali became very ill and the diagnosis of doctors in sundry New York clinics was syphilis. He had, and what an *outré* phonetic similarity, encephalitis, sleeping sickness. He returned to Italy; McAlmon and Ethel Moorehead, who always had their pockets open for the illuminati of the muses, sent him money. I was so enthralled by *A Hurried Man* that I went to Bazzano, a hilly medieval town, two and a half hours by steam train from Bologna, to visit him.

In London I had talked about Carnevali and Walsh and McAlmon and

Herrmann, and these were my first oracles. I had that same awe in meeting these libidinous archangels of vision that Pausanias describes when he saw the lump of clay Prometheus used in moulding the first man. Later in London I spoke to Edith Sitwell about my dear friend, Carnevali, and she asked me whether she could not read *A Hurried Man*. I had also told her of his terrible affliction. Shortly afterwards I was asked to call for the volume, which had become a leper she would not handle, for she feared that she would be infected by *A Hurried Man*. She never was.

In the same tradition as the others, Carnevali disappeared, and the last apocryphal word I had of him was that he was playing the organ in the Vatican.

After leaving Italy I returned to Paris — to the Dôme, the Select, and the Coupole. There was no place else to go. One night I sat at the Coupole until three in the morning with Hart Crane and the quondam surgeon Djuna Barnes describes in *Nightwood*. The doctor told tales of underground sins on the Barbary Coast of San Francisco that were as fabulous as Ophir. He spoke of tars habited as women and with such names as Hazel Dawn and Eve Fig, Eve signifying the serpent and Fig being the symbol of the womb. When I left the Coupole the surgeon held my hand closely in his and, telling me what innocent teeth I had, made a proposal which I declined with punctilio.

Shortly afterwards I had occasion to talk again to Hart Crane at the Cafe de Deux Magots. He had sorrows buried twenty thousand fathoms deep. At twenty-nine he had marine gray hair, a face that was as harmonious as Pythagorean numbers, and the frosty eyes he had ascribed to that other mariner of American literature in the marvelous poem, "At Melville's Tomb." Both Melville and Crane were boreal men seeking the mild trade winds. They were water poets. Melville sought to steep all the ills of his life in the gore of a warm-blooded mammal, the whale, and Hart Crane leaped from a ship, while returning from Mexico, to give himself to the sharks.

Let those who flee from bitter men consider this: Melville and Crane were gentle, cold men, wrapped in seven layers of gall, but with souls that are as tender eating as young pullets.

One afternoon Crane asked me to go with him to the atelier of a friend. There I found myself in the midst of an altercation, and I was startled when I heard Crane say: "Eugene, dear, you ought not to talk to me in that way." He wept, pushing me aside so that he could rush out into the dusk of Paris. His friend gave me his coat saying, "Follow him, or else he will catch cold." I pursued Crane through the twining streets of Montparnasse, his coat dangling from my arm. At one of the *ponts* on the Seine I reached him. He stooped to arrange one of his garters, and turning his suffering face toward me, said: "I guess you think I'm immoral because I am homosexual?" I had already read *White Buildings*, easily his best work, as well as *The Bridge* in manuscript, which he had asked me to do, and I felt that such a poet could not have faults.

Helping him get into his jacket as though I hoped this might be a carapace in which he could hide, I left him; he would always be naked, for only those who are in perpetual want can enter the kingdom of feeling. He returned to his hotel room, and I walked alone down the Boulevard Raspail, thinking that the greater part of our morality comes from a lack of self-knowledge; does not man love his own ordure though he is disgusted at the sight of another's?

What a disorderly animal man is, and how wretched pleasure makes him. Many have died coughing, but not without having derived some marvelous sensation from it. Man is a species of crocodile who does not relish his goodness or his vices unless they are half rotten.

This was the time when the Parisians held every American responsible for the tragic execution of Sacco and Vanzetti. One evening at the Coupole Hart Crane was drunk and began roaring: "Down with France." He was standing at the bar when the waiter behind the counter douched him with seltzer water. Had the waiter known that Hart Crane was the first poet of his country, he might have been even more savage.

Crane threw a lump of traveler's checks on the counter and, after looking about him, picked up a chair to hurl at the bartender. Then three gendarmes arrived; the defender of the honor of France had called the police. When Crane turned toward the door and saw them with clubs in their hands he ran toward them swinging the chair. I stepped between Crane and the three police, knowing that these warped guardian angels of the state would take him to jail and there beat and mangle him, as was done some months later.

Gathering together all of his traveler's checks, I asked him to give me all of his money too, which he meekly did; I feared they would be lost or stolen from him. The gendarmes stood by as I got him into a cab. The following day I returned everything to him.

What little I had done for him had mitigated some obscure pain in me, for that part of us we do not use for others clogs our fate. I had been an inmate of an orphanage in Cleveland when Hart Crane was a soda fountain clerk in his father's fancy ice cream parlor in that city. Crane's establishment was on Euclid Avenue, Plutus's boulevard in Cleveland where John D. Rockefeller and Charles M. Schwab had their great mansions. On the rare occasions when I walked down Euclid Avenue, which smelt of Lake Erie and the windswept money of Troy, I wondered whether I would ever be rich enough to buy one of Crane's ice cream sodas.

Later, when I returned to America, I saw him a few times at his apartment on Columbia Heights which overlooked the Brooklyn Bridge, that stygian iron symbol Crane thought represented the energy of Terra Incognita. There was always a gallon of whiskey and a pile of Sophie Tucker records near his bed. By then he was a fissured Doctor Faustus, burning up in his own crucible of lusts. He ran mad for sailors on the wharves of Lethe at Red Hook, and was beaten to pieces many times in lurid Greenpoint saloons. He complained to me that a street Arab he had taken to his apartment had stolen most of his clothes.

There was a brief and hapless sojourn in Mexico, and one feeble attempt to recover some moiety of Aztec ritual, the old Quetzalcoatl rubbish, for more poems. His whole salt grief lay in those tedious calms between books. He was certain that his powers had ebbed and he feared more than anything else, as Melville had, that he would drown in shoals. A poet is dead when he is not writing, and only a spectre of another age and clime when he is. Writing is done in a moonlit sleep; Isis, Jacob, Joseph, Melville, and Hart Crane were fed by the moon, for of such ore are dreams made.

His life was tragical Dadaism; it was absurd superficially. After his riotous nights in Paris he spent a summer at his father's resort: Crane's Canary Cottage, Chagrin Falls, Ohio. He was so embarrassed when he gave this address to friends that he rented an anonymous post office box.

The last ironic days with his mother cannot be overlooked either. An epicene sister of science and health, she was not averse to flirtations with her son with whom she went dancing when they were together in California. With a mother who was a Christian Science Agrippina, no wonder that Hart Crane knelt before an iron leviathan, the Brooklyn Bridge.

The lives of all these exiled saints of Billingsgate will always attract me enormously, because vice is more interesting than mediocre goodness, and I do not know of any other kind. These men I knew and loved were not bad persons, they simply were not bourgeois. Baudelaire had declared: "I prefer bad people who know what they are doing to these honest folk."

I salute these men; for though now dead they cure my own life; only the deceased can save us.

FOR SALE

GENIUS, LIKE TRUTH, has a shabby and neglected mien. Our poets — the sea-vagabond Melville, the impecunious Quaker Whitman, Thoreau the pencil-maker, Anderson the Ohio town newsboy, and Dreiser the poor Hoosier — came from seedy families. Their books have the character of the oceanic fallow, of sumac, or a wooden river hamlet. The raiment of a book is poverty and the winds. A poet comes to the city to get his thoughts published, but there is always in him some wild Platte, Dakota, or Rocky Mountain peak to resist the simpering vices of trade and deceit. Writing is conscience, scruple, and the farming of our ancestors. Conscience should not be belittled in these times in which virtue must beg pardon of vice as Hamlet tells. Those who write for lucre or fame are grosser Iscariots than the cartel robbers, for they steal the genius of the people, which is its will to resist evil.

Those who are venal debauch and starve the people's mind. The subtlest of foxes give fame only to the dead whose real truths they denied when they lived. Recognize the cunning man not by the corpses he pays homage to but by the living writers he conspires against with the most shameful weapon, Silence, or the briefest review. Hardly a book of human worth, be it heaven's own secret, is honestly placed before the reader; it is either shunned, given a Periclean funeral oration in a hundred and fifty words, or interred in the potter's field of the newspapers' back pages.

The Poet has always been a mendicant and his labors for his country have been scorned or denied. The earnings of a poet could be reckoned by a metaphysician rather than a bookkeeper. Edmund Spenser, writing the epitaph for Thomas Churchyard, Elizabethan versifier, said, "Poverty and poetry this tomb doth inclose." Spenser, himself, died broken and impoverished, but was straightway buried in Westminster Abbey. There are some miserable ironies regarding the fate of authors. There was Stowe, who had exhausted his patrimony doing a remarkable study of English antiquities; in his old age literary James the First permitted him to gather alms from "Our loving subjects." Isaac D'Israeli tells us that the price of a dedication for a play was fixed at five to ten guineas from the Revolution to George I, and from then on twenty. Despite such droll and dismal facts a patron was far better than the foundation whose philisters have none of the learning or wit of the ancient Athenian courtesans who often gave handsome sums of money to Greek writers.

Ibsen said that what is important is not to define literature but to oppose those who are against it. The greatest foes of poems and novels are those in the elite writing business: the Sunday newspaper book editors and the preposition and adjective friars of the universities. The former hawk books as if they were goods, the latter as if they were parts of speech. The text and the gospel of each is FOR SALE. The lives of our poets read like worn-out epitaphs, which can no longer be deciphered. The *New York Times* carried a four-line obituary notice of Herman Melville. We know what pitchy bitterness there was in Melville; at thirty-seven he was already writing his senilia, *The Confidence Man*, which is the Lear of the novel of cheated trust. Without confidence, man crawls away to die in a room or in a book. The pallbearers of the living books are making a legend and scripture out of *The Confidence Man* and *Bartleby*. The persons in the profitable dead-souls business are pouring out essays and volumes on Henry James, Melville, Whitman, Thoreau, Poe, Emily Dickinson, and Crane. They are a malignant sodality of commercial litterateurs that govern ideas, reputations, renown, and whose index expurgatorious is dictated by bile and mammon.

Take heed of the literary merchant, for it is his nature and vocation to humble the poet; beware of the Parnassian grammar boy, for his venom is everywhere. In the beginning was the Word, and then came grammar and spite. Compare these venal foxes with Ford Madox Ford, who, having empty pockets himself, was a Medici patron of literature. Ford was a fat, jolly Falstaff who would lie, cheat, be a highwayman or cutpurse for a madcap Hal of poetry or the novel. "We are not born for ourselves alone," wrote Cicero.

Some of these men were not always such scullions of the Nine Fatal Sisters; Edmund Wilson, as literary editor of the *New Republic,* nothing but a casket magazine today, lampooned such trade hacks as Gorham B. Munson, but more recently he routed Louis Bromfield in some three thousand words. Who now, two to three lustra later, can even identify this scribbler? Horace Gregory was an obscure Milwaukee boy who hated obese, feculent fraud in the early thirties. Like the Roman emperor Tiberius, who studied to be ambiguous, he wrote such a dissembling review on the Trappist monk, Merton, that the publisher was able to pluck a laureled encomium out of it. Trilling, crony of Fadiman, coney-catcher for the Book-of-the-Month Club, was always protean water. Trilling, who writes very badly, discovered that Dreiser also had the same defect; however, this similar flaw does not make them kin. Dreiser had many large, fertile faults, but Trilling only has one which is that he writes. As for Rahv, the sweeper and the beadle of the *Partisan Review*, he has not changed; he is more ignorant than he was in 1930 because he has had thirty years in which to develop.

How important have books been to the republic? Many think that we are not a reading people, and yet the Bible was the loam of the nation in its colonial inception. Rousseau, the French physiocrats, Christian and economic utopians had a marked effect upon the people. Shakespeare was a staple in what was a hoe, rake, and potato commonweal. Fourier, Essene doctrine, and Proudhon were avidly read by Shakers, Mennonites, Oneidans, and the rest of that astonishing band of dissidents that established their various cults in America beginning in 1830 and continuing down through the seventies.

What has happened since then? The printing press has become the devil in the land; we are no longer a nation of readers though more words are published here than in the rest of the world. The mammon press and book gossip have taken the place of the New Testament and Shakespeare.

The average American hates negations, imagining that darksome, angered words are just for pests and renegades, but little do the many know that we have been a nation of dissidents since our outpost beginnings. Read the books of the late nineteenth-century authors: Mrs. R. H. Davis, first of the mordant realists, who wrote "Life in the Iron Mills," Hamlin Garland's *Main Travelled Roads*, Edgar Howe's *Story of a Country Town*, Edward Eggleston's *The Circuit Rider*, Joseph Kirkland's *Zury*, Henry B. Fuller's *With the Procession* and *The Cliff-Dwellers*. One will garner from these local-color books none of that purblind hysteria which is making us automobile barbarians and a nation evilly cursed by actors, or what Plato called the vileness of a theatocracy.

What has become of the truth-and-vision cranks, like Whitman, or the libertarian, Henry B. Tucker, or Victoria Woodhull, or Eugene Debs? In the past fifty years the thinking rebel, so essential to the spinal vitality of the nation, has disappeared or been lost. Sherwood Anderson was an American grotesque, an agrarian apostle whose father was a harness-maker, and whose language was close to oats, barley, and horses; his books remind us of the horses in Swift's *Gulliver* in whose speech there was no word for falsehood. Anderson's thwarted heroes — an Ohio telegrapher, a farmer-inventor, a washing-machine manufacturer — brood like Job and act like Solomon. Dreiser had come out of Terre Haute, like the Nazarene socialist Debs from the same city; both men had urgent need of books, without which they felt their lives were ugly and perverted. They were meditative men who considered the dogwood, the branches, and the humble.

Have these malcontents vanished from the American earth? Anderson and Dreiser were both book-readers who happened to write; they were the Matthew's salt of our literature. The writer and the reader are very far apart, and this is a malady in both. Our alphabet is no longer love; the word has become a private code of the spirit. Gibbon, in his *Decline and Fall of the Roman Empire*, states that the use of letters is the principal characteristic which distinguishes a civilized people from a herd of savages. Compare the *Popol Vuh*, Mayan sacred writings, with our sick alphabet literature or with base newspaper language, and it is apparent that we are not becoming more simple and sane but more lunatic and squalid. Speech, to be a deity to the people, must come from the pasture or from grain, fruits, and livestock. We must not forget that the simple is not only not mean or obvious but has in it such depths and gods as to be a healing medicine for the soul, the body, and the earth. The earth, too, is suffering from man's spleen, greed, and malice. Is it credible that no more than five hundred to a thousand readers can be obtained for Randolph Bourne's *Untimely Papers*, or that a little volume of verse, Anderson's *A New Testament*, a lamb of Christ and lust, can have no audience? Who can believe that up until recently there was no need to reissue Stephen Crane's short stories of the mesa and the Rio Grande? Until lately the only complete edition of Melville's works was done in 1921 by Constable in London.

We have had some gallant publishers. Duyckinck introduced Shakespeare to a sailor named Herman Melville. Foremost among the later American publishers was Ben Huebsch, who was one of the cavalier gentlemen of taste with a civil regard for American letters. For him, as for the late Thomas Seltzer, the Boni brothers, Horace Liveright, the early Harcourts, and Pascal Covici, publishing was a grace. An enumeration of the many Huebsch titles is itself a vision of an American Pisgah. Huebsch was Sherwood Anderson's first publisher, having brought out *Windy McPherson's Son*, *Marching Men*, *Winesburg, Ohio*, *The Triumph of the Egg*, *Many Marriages*, and *A Story-Teller's Story*. There were the two volumes of the valiant Randolph Bourne, *Untimely Papers* and *The History of a Literary Radical*, and the one poetic novel Jules Romains ever did, *The Death of a Nobody*. Sorel's *Reflections on Violence* was also on Huebsch's list, and he published James Joyce's *The Portrait of the Artist as a Young Man*, when English printers feared to do it, besides Joyce's *Dubliners*. There were *Chekov's Notebook* and Gorki's little masterpiece, *Remembrances of Leo Tolstoi*, which I gave to two ardent admirers of it, Theodore Dreiser and Alfred Stieglitz. Besides, he printed the original *Freeman* for four years, as important to American culture as *Seven Arts*, the *Dial*, *Pagany*, *Contempo*, *This Quarter*, *Transition*, and the *Little Review*. Horace Liveright was the friend of American genius, publishing Dreiser, Anderson, Hart Crane's *White Buildings* and *The Bridge*. Pascal Covici in Chicago printed the *Literary Times* where Anderson and Emanuel Carnevali could write; Covici was the first to bring out the imagist poet, Richard Aldington. Seltzer issued D. H. Lawrence's *Studies in Classical American Literature* which had been in limbo for so many years and is one of the few works on Crèvecoeur, Hawthorne, Melville, Poe, and Whitman with human wisdom.

Money-cynics report that these men did not do well, but it is a fact that they lived with a gallant *élan* and that the marvelous volumes they printed were food for them. These men are princes of the republic, and the debt owed them can only be weighed in Job's Honest Scales.

The patron too has disappeared; foundations are extremely reluctant to give a poet or a man of letters a grant. These institutions generally give awards to academic boobs and syllabus simians to do research work on the use of the nominative case in colonial documents. Neither Dreiser, Bourne, Anderson, nor Williams ever received money from the Guggenheim Foundation. Vachel Lindsay was refused an award by the Guggenheim Foundation which is guided solely by the American factory cult of youth because he was fifty-one. Amiel said that no one could regard himself as a writer until he was fifty.

Who is the prey of the book columnists? The reader, the poet, the publisher. There is not space to jot down the many rare volumes having an underground fame that were ignored by the papers and magazines. The truth is that an author with windmills in his head cannot read a book column without Gulliver's nausea. Mention a volume of verse to a publisher now and he regards it as a sinister intimation. The patrons in this century have been the writers themselves, Ford Madox Ford, and Herbert Read.

Who will impede ambition, the evil angel that fleers at feeling and the thirsting heart? Who will stand between the guileless reader and the newspaper which whets the vilest appetites it feigns to quell? Remy de Gourmont once wrote that as long as people read newspapers they would not read books, and Tolstoi and Arthur Symons and Upton Sinclair have repeated the same desolate truths. Dreiser once told me that what we need is not freedom of the press, but freedom from it. What will happen to the Cana wine poems? and how can the reader learn what is a cankered, venal volume and what is honest? We know that there is little chance for the poor, humble book, for the touchstone of the papers is news. The whole Ezra Pound legend is craven gossip; two decades ago Pound was so neglected that he sent his death mask to the *New York Times* to see what kind of an obituary he would receive. Only when Pound became a fascist and a virulent Jew-baiter and was committed to an asylum was he an Achilles in the newspapers. Ford Madox Ford, when he had been dead a decade, was portrayed in the *Times* as an obese eunuch who had no sexual or intellectual perils for a girls' school. The mocking presumption is that the reader is without analytic faculty. Years ago Upton Sinclair published at his own expense a socialist denunciation of newspaper book-suppression which he called *Money Writes*. These same papers, posing as the Ariel of the spirit, are always clamoring about censorship.

Why is it that the most invidious hack is chosen to write about a seer? Do we go to Pilate to comprehend Jesus, or ask Herod to judge St. John whom he beheaded? This is the rabble practice of the magazines and the papers. Russian papers often had columns by Tolstoi or Dostoevski. It was Dostoevski who was the first to announce that Tolstoi would be of world-wide importance. Chekov gave the young, green Gorki counsel and comfort; Frank Norris came to the defense of the lonely Dreiser. Joshua Kunitz told me Gorki had wept on so many vests over new geniuses he had discovered that someone suggested a Gorki vest museum be founded. What paper or magazine has been the valorous Gideon of American genius? What real, obscure talent has Mark Van Doren, a crump ephor of our dollar literati, announced in his whole lifetime? Edmund Wilson and the grammar boys of Parnassus, Trilling and Horace Gregory, have given prodigal encouragement to Matthew Arnold, Henry James, Pope, Gogol, Sophocles and the sacred writers of Genesis. In 1930 I mentioned Lawrence's *Studies in Classical American Literature* to a scoffing Edmund Wilson, who has since then included the entire volume in *The Shock of Recognition.*

Wise books are not property for the moneychangers of the human spirit who are always prating about the suppression of free ideas and truths abroad. Why, our own books are outcast, underground literature! We have genius, the living waters, and it is not all dead like James, Whitman, Melville, Dickinson, and Crane, whom we honor; the people are entitled to the living miracles, without which we are all blind, crippled, and palsied at Bethesda, for a true book is the opening of the eyes and the healing of the halt and the blind.

The attention given to debris and to evil volumes and the almost uniform neglect and murder of genius reminds one of the priest who ran out into the streets on St. Bartholomew's night crying, "Kill everybody, God will protect the innocent." Without the vigilant aid of readers, what can God do against Irita Van Doren? Our whole culture hangs together by the slender thread of Ariadne, and the readers along with the publisher must demand that the *Herald Tribune*, the *New York Times*, the *New Republic*, that sham-radical rag the *New York Evening Post*, and even more oleaginous in their practices than these, the *Partisan Review*, and the grammar monks, be honest and undouble about those books which are more than the raiment and the meat.

PEOPLELESS FICTION

WHAT IS MOST APPALLING in an F. Scott Fitzgerald book is that it is *peopleless* fiction: Fitzgerald writes about spectral, muscled suits; dresses, hats, and sleeves which have some sort of vague, libidinous throb. These are plainly the products of sickness. A farm road, a glebe, a plain, and an elm breed charity and pity, which the fiction of groundless city surfeit and nausea lacks. There is nothing left in the urban, peopleless novel but the national smirk, and that is what the billboard eye of the oculist in *The Great Gatsby* really is. It is the closest that Fitzgerald ever came to seeing the human eye.

I realize that judgments about books are very perilous, that he who has written a book should not cast the first stone. But what I am most troubled about is not being right or wrong about the small talent of this deceased author, but the almost gaping admiration of our contemporaries for his books. This is a baleful sign of a puling American volition; also, alas, of a great deal of lying about reputations by people who cannot write but who want above all to be known as authors.

We have had many subhuman journalistic novels acclaimed because they are true "facts," although they are without moral reflection, learning, or compassion. The newspaper has debauched the American until he is a slavish, simpering, and angerless citizen; it has taught him to be a lump mass-man toward fraud, simony, murder, and lunacies more vile than those of Commodus or Caracalla. Our torpid, prurient annals of brutish evils do not lead ordinary people to meditation or moral indignation. Has either Hitler or Stalin done more to injure human ideals and volition than the chronicles of our front-page crimes?

The Great Gatsby is newspaper realism about a Long Island hamlet called West Egg. West Egg is one of many thousands of automat Sunday towns — lawned, bungalowed, but unpeopled until Friday night. Gatsby has a large mansion, a swimming pool, a Rolls Royce, all of which are utterly spectral except for weekends when they are filled with dancing, gyrating suits and gowns.

Everybody in a Fitzgerald book is denatured, without parents or family, for the mortuary home has taken the place of the old frame house with porch, weedy steps, a clothesline in the yard. Tom Buchanan, athlete with polo ponies and a big automobile, is married to Daisy, the perennial vestal spinster. They have a modern utilitarian relationship based on the most subhuman inertia; their marriage reminds us of our conveniences in comfort, fruits, and self-service. Seedless grapes, seedless oranges, seedless wedlock all go together; in a cafeteria marriage like Tom Buchanan's, a dreary, enervated husband casually helps himself to his wife, for nobody wants to bother about anything any longer. The more inventions we have, the more apathetic we are toward others.

In the peopleless realism of Fitzgerald the author appears to have no role in the narrative. For the sake of a humbug objectivity the novelist becomes as dingy, as depleted, and as seedless as the objects and the deanimated persons in the book. The Fitzgerald men are effete male ingenues, brutish and shrewd, like Stahr in *The Last Tycoon*. Tom Buchanan breaks his wife's nose because he is an athlete and has to do something with his body.

We have today a novel that is very weak in locality, wisdom, sex, and people. Human beings, still ranging the megalopolitan cement savannas, are almost as extinct as the bison. The amorous novels of Dreiser and Anderson have been replaced by a very tired fiction. The old Don Juan blood is graveled, the eye no longer riots, the ear is torpid. The Byronic petard has given way to simpering, senile lewdness. When a book is implacably dull we are told that this was the intention of the author, and when the hero is a great bore or is a colossus of idiocy we are advised that this is the representative American. Josephine Herbst writes of the sickness in the novel "where the worms are stroked with loving."

Fitzgerald's fiction is filled with slovenly writing. Such loose slopping of prose is considered good simply because it is done in the vernacular. Let me quote some of Fitzgerald: "complexion powdered milky white," "Mrs. Wilson . . . looked at us with a brilliant smile," "My heart was fire, and smoke was in my eyes and everything," "something gorgeous" about Gatsby, "friendly trees," "dried-up little blond," "her glowing beauty and her unexplored novelty," "a twinkling blur for Santa Monica," "the California moon was out, huge and orange over the Pacific," "the padded hush of tires, the quiet tick of a motor," "my stomach dipped a little at the proximity to Stahr," "the stewardess . . . tall, handsome, and flashing dark." These are just meager samples of the grim banalities in *Gatsby*, *Tender Is the Night*, *The Last Tycoon*. Whitman, Norris, Crane, Hamlin Garland, and Dreiser wrote a bluff barbaric vulgate which is sometimes very nimble and very manly. Their words, deriving from the old, manual occupations, are far more masculine and energetic than the lymphatic ones that come from advertising and from inventions that are emasculating the human faculties. A word that arouses some sort of contemplative or physical activity is good, and one that does not is base. I don't care for forceless platitudes (even though they are employed by most of the people) any more than I do for cheating, stealing, lying, or murder. Dreiser's definition of virtue in *Sister Carrie* as caring for others, is a sane credo for writing; a book weak in human affections and which nourishes effeminacy and apathy, not caring for other people, is baneful. I like also to see men in love with women in a novel; I have scant patience with the Fitzgerald athlete, the "blond, spiritless man," or a "gorgeous" Gatsby.

It is perhaps a tragedy for a writer to have come from — or even to — the eastern cities. New York is the big placeless Acheron, where locality, entirely protean, is always being mangled, and where nothing comes to rest. Everything rolls in the rubber-tire cities; indeed, the whole motor-car country is rapidly becoming East — and that is a dismal carnage for our literature and people. Hamlin Garland quit Boston to return to Wisconsin; Sherwood Anderson is insubstantial whenever he departs from the cornfields, the harness shop, and the asparagus beds of Ohio. What would have become of the genius of Dreiser had he not been a Hoosier? We are a wild beast people given to the dingiest rootless violences when we live in the slag cities; we have no way then of comprehending the Sierras, the vast inland sea-prairies, or the Rockies in us. Our faculties are at their best when they are not subtle or shrewd, for we are only brothers to one another on the scathed Dakota plains, or in the old middle border region. We have become sick animals, devouring others because we are rootless. I doubt that we will ever be an intellectual nation: we are so miserable in times of peace that we are always going to war as the substitute for the vanishing mesa, the distant buttes, the great Rockies, which are as remote in our lives as sunken Atlantis. The American is never quiet, and his literature is prairie and river geography, unsocial and nomadic, like Melville's leviathan, Twain's Mississippi, the mesa of Crane, Norris's Mojave and Hamlin Garland's Middle Border. Our literature lacks maxims and proverbs; cartography takes the place of the intellectual faculty.

I have the scantiest regard for our nineteenth-century grammar sextons, Woodberry, Higginson, Stoddard, Stedman, and Rufus Griswold. But far worse than these foes of American genius is Dr. Ha'penny Knowledge who calls Fitzgerald a Goethean nature. Such a remark is likely to leave even a man of wit either senseless or dead, or, at least, unfit for combat. The new academic refers to Fitzgerald's notebook, *The Crack-Up*, as memorabilia, foxily drawing the reader's mind to Xenophon's account of Socrates. One would imagine that this is the end of the funereal praise, but then the academic tradesman of the muses informs us that Fitzgerald had abundant modesties. To prove this he tells us that when Fitzgerald was criticized, he bashfully defended himself by comparing *The Great Gatsby* with *The Brothers Karamazov*. Miguel de Unamuno tells us: "It is time to call a fool a fool, a liar a liar, and a thief a thief."

When everybody wants to paint or write, the arts are very bad. If Lionel Trilling really loved literature he would stop writing. When a critic admires so bad a writer as Fitzgerald, he is simply confessing that he himself cannot write. Dr. Ha'penny Knowledge is too ambitious: as Dr. Emil G. Conason says, what ails him is literacy, which is fast becoming a national malady.

CHIVERS AND POE

THE SMALL LIFE OF POE by Dr. Thomas Holley Chivers was perhaps finished in 1857, a year before Chivers' death, and has been mummified in the Huntington Library until recently. As an ode in prose to Poe, it is false, orphic sublimity, but the homage is tender and just and comes from a quick, interior nature alien to gross matter. Despite the biographies of Poe, and his current revivification, the author of "The Raven" still stands as a great, ruined obelisk in American literature. His genius is a monumental waste; his marvelous tales, gothic cabala, are transhuman and inscrutable.

Chivers has left us some swollen dithyrambs on Poe's person. "The Messiah of melody," as Chivers describes his hero, had a pensive, Grecian bend when he walked, and a long, slender neck which made him appear taller when seated. Poe had feminine hands and considerable knowledge in the "aesthetics of dress." He carried a cane, and I imagine he would have worn the vests of Bacchus or Heinrich Heine, or been as modish as Baudelaire, if he had possessed the money. Chivers' remark that money would have ruined Poe shows abundant wisdom, for though many writers have been harmed by penury, more have suffered damage from lucre.

Poe gave readings to ladies' societies dedicated to gabbling. He had a chaste voice, but he lacked the humbug actor's inflections needed for success in such groups. He was very vain, as all good writers are (the meek ones are furtive, belonging to another tribe). He had told Chivers that every article in the last number of the *Broadway Journal* was remarkable and had been written by himself, with the exception of one poem which Chivers claimed was also by Poe. Poe had a testy temperament, an occupational trait of the writer, but he also had a good digestion, which Chivers asserts is not a scholarly sign.

Emily Dickinson had no one to turn to except that drab ecclesiastic of letters, Thomas Wentworth Higginson, who was astonished at the reception the posthumous publication of her verse received. Poe, no less unfortunate than Miss Dickinson, had as his literary executor the Reverend Rufus Griswold. Griswold wrote a memoir about Poe which in pure weight of spite took care of the same amount of genius Griswold lacked. This stygian piece of literary Calvinism endured, and for a hundred years what has concerned the attention of exsanguine critics was Poe's drunkenness. There was also small pardon in the ashy hearts of the critics for the poet's marriage to Virginia Clemm, his cousin, when she was thirteen.

Along with Rufus Griswold and the other predatory prudes on lower Broadway who could not abide Poe's rancor or his astonishing abilities was Margaret Fuller. A rude, bellicose crone of the arts, Miss Fuller got up a delegation which demanded that Mrs. Osgood relinquish Poe's friendship!

There were other recondite scandals in Poe's life. He had had a fugitive liaison with one of the lady poets of the time. Eros is cold and altogether reposeful in the "Tales," though Poe was a toady to any Ophelia. He could pen a frightening invective against almost any man who malpracticed verse, but he was the serpent and dove with the lady poetasters. Poe found in many of these dear sibyls, whose sighs were more beatific than their poems, the most valorous defenders of his character and afflatus. There were Sarah Helen Whitman, Mrs. Osgood, and Emilie Weltby who had pulsed to Poe's genius and manners and august face. Maria Clemm, the mother of his bride, loved her two occult children, and Mrs. R. S. Nichols, another defender, wrote the monody, "let him rest by lost 'Lenore.'"

"Israfel" was a greater original than Byron, Shelley, or Keats. Poe's verse is very inferior to Keats's "Hyperion" or to the "Endymion," but the form of Poe's prose poems is aboriginal. He was an abstruse psalmist, a saturnine Saul who had stature of soul. "Ligeia," "Eleonora," "Berenice," "The Fall of the House of Usher," are Arabic music of the soul fit for an Antony or the seraglio in Mahomet's Paradise, but of what profit to human wisdom or to the spirit in its transient, purblind earthly pilgrimage? Chivers said of Poe that he "always wrote as though all Poetry consisted more in the Poetry of the language than in the passions of the heart to be expressed through that language."

Without Poe's "Tales," *Les Fleurs du Mal* could not have been born in Baudelaire's mind. Each morning before starting to write, Baudelaire prayed to the Virgin Mary, to his mother, and to Edgar Poe. That poems should be cold, passionless objectivism is the creed of the imagists, who, in part, are the heirs of Poe. The "Tales" are flowers in hell, and they have the odor of Persephone. It is with the most obdurate reluctance that I suggest that they are the fallen angelic parent of today's cankered mystery story. Poe's belief that a poem ought to be governed by the ratiocinative intellect rather than by the controlled tumult of feeling has been taken up by today's Brahmins of aesthetics. Poe so hated the forerunners of these Brahmins, the mandarins of Beacon Hill of the nineteenth century, that he always said he was born in Baltimore, though his birthplace was actually in Boston.

There were some arguments between Poe and Chivers. Poe admired some of Lowell's verse; Chivers thought Poe had overpraised Lowell. Poe regarded Tennyson as a great bard; Chivers regarded him as "a phlegmatic fat baby." Sharing Chivers' feeling, James Joyce called the poet "Alfred Lawn Tennyson."

Dr. Chivers was a marvelous friend, for he was a poet himself. (Cézanne once said that it takes one writer to catch another.) Chivers did not have to wait a century to be an enthusiast of a contemporary genius. He wrote: "I allude . . . to those who dispraised him in his lifetime, on account of envy of his genius, as well as to those still more despicable souls who pretend to defend him on the still basic principle of wishing the world to believe that they are . . . the faithful Apostles of his greatness." Any writer reading this prayer cannot help but say in his own conceited heart, "I wish that Dr. Thomas Holley Chivers had known me!"

CUTPURSE PHILOSOPHER

WILLIAM JAMES WAS AN ACADEMIC PARADOX; he was a sparse man and a lifelong neurasthenic who was also the Chautauquan evangelist of health and energy. He had a summer home in New Hampshire with fourteen doors, all opening outward, as he said. James hated the desiccated pedagogue upon whom he has had such an enormous influence. For all of his plain extroversions he was, perhaps, a *sub rosa* cutpurse philosopher who not only took from Charles Peirce the word "pragmatism," but Peirce's doctrine. Peirce, unable to get a university appointment because he was supposed to be a rough and thorny nature, had tombstone reticences, and never attacked his friend James as a plagiarist. A lonely man, who used odd and bare-rock words, Peirce was, however, sufficiently vexed with James to change "pragmatism" to "pragmaticism."

The main fault with pragmatic thought is its language. Peirce's words are isolated and austere and have a dry Nantucket vision about them, but James's books are glutted with those gregarious, yokel phrases that have become the shibboleths of specious educators. The ancient Greek philosophers paid a great deal of attention to their hexameters, and it is still very doubtful that bad writing can be the groundwork of philosophical speculation. Once John Dewey wrote that it was not necessary for science to be dull, unmindful that his own books are all written in a nasal monotone.

James's slack prose has got many an American author into much moral trouble, for it is the ethical judgments of the pragmatic thinkers that are most ambiguous. This equivocation was a source of great concern to Charles Peirce. James's hatred of principles and abstractions made him an apostle of expediency. Though James was religious, there was no evening in his soul. Despite his skepticism regarding absolutes, he said that there was in human experience an internal "push" against which man is powerless, but which impels him toward ends, or what he called the "destiny of our belief."

It was easy enough for James to attack the fluxional principles of science, but do morals really change? Do we read the Socratic dialogues with a different ethical nature than Plato had when he wrote them? William James was a foe of Royce, who said that the existence of God rested upon the existence of evil. What irritated James most was Royce's explanation of human vice, which somehow or other is translated into the good of God. But, as we know, James believed the results of an idea determine its human value, and this is very dangerous political doctrine (it was Mussolini who told Eduard Lindeman that pragmatism was the father of fascism). James's theories fathered the kind of American education that has been doctored by the academic and exchequer Poloniuses of social adjustment.

No matter what the advocates of William James say, if his books are read with searching honesty, it will be very difficult to deny that pragmatism is a credo for men with equivocal ends in mind.

RANDOLPH BOURNE

THERE IS NOTHING like Tolstoi's essays and letters on a human commonwealth save Randolph Bourne's *Untimely Papers*. There is less cult and American geography in Bourne, the hunchback from Bloomfield, New Jersey, than in any other of our writers. He died at thirty-two in 1918, and did not have time to feel the vast, wild weight of American place. Underneath our genius, which is not really political, is the crust of cult, for we turn every doctrine into a Bible, sex, or geographic screed. What Herzen, the nineteenth-century Russian social apostle, said is true of the United States: "Revolution just as reformation stands in the churchyard."

By some kind of stale irony books that were once remaindered frequently become deluxe collector's items. This was the fate of Bourne's *Untimely Papers* and *The History of a Literary Radical*, both published posthumously in 1919 and 1920, never reissued, and now meanly sepulchred in a few large libraries.

Bourne's career is ironic for another reason. The numerous men who acclaimed his intransigent vision, among whom were Van Wyck Brooks,

Lewis Mumford, Waldo Frank, and John Dos Passos, have become today the same kind of sleepy and inert pragmatists that Bourne so valiantly assailed in his own time. By his unseasonable death he seems to have taken from them the force they so needed.

A closer look at his broken body, which had so much will and character in it, is important. Waldo Frank, his friend in the *Seven Arts* days, writes that as an infant he had been dropped: Bourne was five feet tall and had the spindled legs of Pope, another gnome, who used to wrap three pairs of stockings around his calves. Bourne was such a cripple that when he went on a walking tour through the Italian hill towns the peasant women crossed themselves when he passed. He wore a black cape to hide his fate, but also because he was a sensual gypsy Leporello with women. The most sensitive piece about Bourne was written by Dreiser, who tells how he saw a little dwarf, mantled in a black cape, walking through a January snow flurry; his first reaction was not pity but automatic horror, and sidling up against the brick wall of the old Village night court at Eighth Street, he watched the poor, hapless thing pass. Considering for a moment how hard and predatory the human heart is, he soon forgot about the incident altogether. A short time later, the same hunchback came to his door, and in a soft, pulsing voice said that he was an ardent admirer of *The Hoosier Holiday*, and that his name was Randolph Bourne. Here the pity ends, and the one or two acts allowed him as a rebel with gay, male health commences.

Bourne regarded himself as an impossibilist and made the most implacable exactions upon fate. His name, Bourne, meaning end, was ample declaration of his nature and his motives, for he insisted that the path toward the goal is the vision itself, and if the means be evil, the ideal will be a beast. Upon the rock of impossibilism this angry elf stood, flogging the winds and the stars, and hurling his words like Homeric stones at the philosophers of expediency, and in particular at his friend and teacher, John Dewey. He made the accusation that pragmatism is a philosophy for action and not for the waiting contemplative faculty which does not hurry history. For this attack against the "Pragmatic Adjusters," who included Veblen and A. M. Simons as well as Dewey, Bourne was called a diseased deformity by Amy Lowell, who had elephantiasis. Although he had been deeply influenced by Kropotkin, Rousseau, Veblen, and Whitman, Bourne was opposed to the fetish of politics and what he called the "new orthodoxies of propaganda." He believed that, ultimately, politics, the serpent, would devour the word, the image, and the rebel who preserves the spirit of the nation.

There was an unusual amount of animal wisdom in his misshapen body, and the sharp, energetic prophecies in the *Literary Radical* are lessons yet to be learned. Bourne understood the subtlest fiscal paradoxes in American education and philosophy. In the *Literary Radical* there is the portrait of the bursar Polonius, the presidents and professors of our monetary academies of lower learning. One of the sitters in that remarkable book is John Erskine, "the pale timid Gideon," who studies pre-Elizabethan literature and routs philistia by writing a vulgarian's novel about Helen of Troy. Bourne saw the American merchant-scholar getting into easy and comfortable relations with his surroundings. He knew that the pragmatic mind, a votary of bulk culture, what William James called "the cult of the big," would never struggle for crucial, visionary ends, and that all we could hope from it was the philosophy of fatigued acquiescence that so pervades contemporary American civilization.

Bourne's own position was tragic; belonging to that small but dispersed sodality of nomadic iconoclasts he wrote a book that was a bitter, Lear's truth. The writer in America, a banished man unable to dissolve the forlorn cleavage between himself and society, often forsakes the role of the untouchable city anchorite and turns to mammon or to a specious herd scholarship for the social satisfactions denied him by his books. The chameleon radical, as Bourne pointed out, has many natures and methods. The common trend in writing today is the pachydermatous degradation of real values. Higher learning is debased by the perverted academic hack who promiscuously lumps together Tacitus and the scurvy Kinsey report. The guileless reader is duped by the venal college professor who endeavors to persuade him that vision and truth and the churl's book are equal to one another. Randolph Bourne knew that the herd academic mind (and the phrase is his) is no different from the street urchin's intelligence; and now we can say that our universities are no longer monastic cloisters, vapory and remote from the people, but are reflections of our national mammon culture. We fear negations more than any other people, and so we affirm everything to produce a lump character for the nation. We require, as we had in Randolph Bourne, a pen that is a whip; for if the dissident in the land perish, who will be the cup-bearer to Zeus but the instrumentalist and the militant pederastic Ganymede of idealism?

We are today confronted with sundry dilemmas, a possible war with Russia and the perplexing questions answered in *Untimely Papers*. Bourne understood with that wonderful prescience of his that though the state should win the war abroad, the people would be defeated at home. What he required was that the American be vigilant with all his nature, lest the state, like that fabled vulture that tormented Prometheus, win the war and eat the nation's organs. Bourne wrote that the constitution was a *coup d'état* against the people — the farmers, the cordwainers, the artisans — and that the separate states in a loosely federated colony, far from suffering from the lack of central-state mysticism, were flourishing. We see that the doctrines of Alexander Hamilton, the patrician usurer of the nation, have had their ripest expression today and that the Hamiltonian dollar visionaries have pre-empted the farms, the wealth, and the trade of the nation. Bourne's unfinished essay on the state is the most radical piece of writing ever done in America, but it is no different in anger from Thoreau's "Civil Disobedience"; Thoreau always regarded government, whether it be Massachusetts or Washington, as the pickpocket of the nation. And Henry Adams, coming after him, had the greatest uneasiness about the influence of Hamilton who he said was an "adventurer." Bourne was almost alone; only Dreiser and the *Seven Arts* editors were of his mind, with the exception of Van Wyck Brooks who detested Bourne's ideas. Now there are two miserable hazards an intellectual has to take: he finds himself either in the position of advocating patriotism, which Samuel Johnson said was the last refuge of a scoundrel, or he becomes a solitary apostate, and I believe that it is as hard for us to be lonely figures as it was for the ancient Greeks. We know that Socrates, who did not have to take the hemlock and who could have escaped from his cell, would not consider going into exile. Bourne was a banished man, and the one organ, *Seven Arts*, he had in which to articulate his ideas was discontinued because of his essays, "Twilight of Idols" (the attack on John Dewey) and "Below the Battle," both of which are in *Untimely Papers*.

The Department of Justice had confiscated a trunkful of Bourne's manuscripts, and agents from that Department, examining some of Bourne's verse with the gigantic stupor of a Cyclops, thought it was secret code and espionage. Freedom is the shibboleth of a state at war. Wilson the president was an impeccable state-man and he imprisoned Eugene Debs, the Nazarene socialist, for saying nothing more libelous than the truth. His treatment of conscientious objectors, socialists, and Quakers — mostly religious pacifists, and there were no more than about three thousand of them, as Norman Thomas has revealed in a book called *The Conscientious Objector* — reveals his hatred of the dissident. What made it almost unendurable was that the intellectual classes were more hardened enemies of Bourne than the government. His relentless foes were John Dewey and Charles A. Beard, who called him a guttersnipe in the *New Republic*, which shut its book column to him because of his attitude toward a "democratic, antiseptic war." A war intellect is a predatory faculty and the war writers were what Bismarck called "ink beasts." Bourne had said that Dewey, Veblen, Gompers, and A. M. Simons had taken their place alongside the Legion and the vigilantes.

We still admire a Maxim Gorki for having sent letters to other writers in enemy lands, begging them not to succumb to rabble state hatred. The epistles of Romain Rolland will last longer than all his books. Rolland believed that great landmarks — the Louvain library, cathedrals, medieval houses once tenanted by a Petrarch or a Cavalcanti — produce angels in men and are of more importance than the unfortunates on the battlefield; for, as Bourne writes, the craft of the state is war, but the art of the nation is weaving, a Shaker chair, Whitman's cottage in Camden, New Jersey.

The destruction of American peace arts has made us cowards at home and invincible abroad. We are a nation today of auto mechanics, and though I think that Russia will be miserably defeated in a war with the United States, only men with rough state throats can rejoice or peal at such a victory. Conquering Americans will return to their land worse paupers than the Greeks after sacking Troy. We will be conspicuously poor in human learning. Two wars have already made us a land of robbers; we cheat and waste each other; to use a Veblen phrase, waste is our conspicuous ideal. And because it is, we have not yet understood that our strength for war enfeebles our arts, without which we are man-eaters, devouring each other more than our foes. The auto, which has made the American the biggest potential rolling army in the world, has also drained us of that plenitude of quiet and patience that makes a people significant in wisdom rather than in waste.

This is a corrosive, war-nerve culture and not an era of love and human adhesion. The industrial city (a war arsenal and not for homes, the wine-press, marriage, bread) exhausts and stupefies the multitude; the peace-machines themselves are what Bourne describes as the "rotten armaments of war." War is the health of the state, wrote Heraclitus, which Bourne uses as his ironic theme in "The State." "The State is always latently at War," asserted Bourne. Our vast, wild production is the invidious battle material by which we enslave the people at home and defeat the oppressor abroad.

The plough is a sign of peaceable ground-workers, but the rubber tire is a tool of a nomadic, apathetic class that is constantly moving away from debts, marriage, and boredom. The rubber-tire pleb is a factory nihilist whose hopes have been wasted by the great money cynics, the auto and banking patricians. The rubber tire is also a great war wheel, and the token of a vast homeless class, for a city and people on wheels are essentially for going, waste, and battle. A workman who is yoked to a bench all day turning a wheel or riveting a bolt has the nerve-shock for war; factory drudgery has disabled him as a household husband, and has left him with cindered nerves that crave a plenitude of shock which is to be had by divorce — which is house-breaking — or by leaving town — usually some kind of moral skulking — or by going to battle. Going somewhere else is his most exceptional satisfaction.

One of the bitterest paradoxes is that the pawnbroker, once considered the vilest grubworm in a despotic nation, has been given patrician rank in a republican commonwealth. Great wealth is an infamous sin, for there is just so much money in a people's larder, meaning that if a few men have most of the nation's riches, they have obviously got it by stealing the ground, the houses, and the labor of the helpless and more trusting classes, and anyone who denies this is a rogue. One does not have to have a complex economic doctrine to understand that this is true. But how words have changed, and how they have fallen: we are now being told that money-lending is not a vice though it has already eaten up the country's ground, agriculture, homes, and far worse its hopes, which are the moral stamina of a just and good republic of people who are neither rich nor poor. The banking and auto rulers have brought about in the classes they plunder the most derisive attitude toward Thou Shalt Not Cheat, or Mock, or Insult, or Steal from Thy Neighbor.

There are no just wars; the "rough, rude currents of health" which come from war enervate all classes, for any war is a fierce animal wound that stings the populace into madness. No intellectual can urge a people to go into battle without impairing his own faculties; for the war mind, as Bourne wrote, is the herd intellect, and if there be any doubt about this look at the martial writings of Henry James, Thorstein Veblen, or John Dewey. The American, to repeat, does not have political genius; and though he is the best auto-soldier in the world, he returns home to sack the peace with as much fury as Achilles pillaged cities.

The American is at best a Bible and sex utopian. Walt Whitman's *Leaves of Grass* is marvelous crank verse on human physiology, and it is no accident that Whitman's disciple was Horace Traubel, the Christian anarchist, who was also the biographer of Eugene Debs. Debs, far from being the wage apostle, was a Sermon-on-the-Mount man, and had a great deal of knowledge about American Bible rebels, like the Shakers, the

Oneidans, and Rapp's Harmony Society. It is no random matter either that Henry Wallace, burning crops and porkers to relieve the American of unclean abundance, was the friend of Sherwood Anderson, the remarkable lust-cult poet of America. The trade-unionists are, as Josephine Herbst once very accurately remarked, dinner-pail apostles of wages, hours, and comfort — the three beasts that today are together devouring Conscience, Honesty, and Justice. The lodestar of the trade-unionist is apathy, and his indifference to the people is as cynical as that of the money Borgia, the college professor, and the writer. The ancient prophet weighed the egg as carefully as he did the law, knowing that unjust prices ruin and loot the law, the spirit, the wine, and the oil of the people. Do the trade unions, the professors, or the poets go out like angry Gideons to combat thieves, usury, cartels, milk at twenty-three cents a quart or beef at a dollar-ten a pound? The nation has become booty, and no one advises the impotent people punished by thievish prices and draconian taxes, that what matters most is not the auto pleb, the college professor, or the writer, but good workmanship, learning, and literature.

There is a great deal of humbug in American genius, which is likely to break out in table-rapping, mind-reading, and such clairvoyant perplexities as were so deep in William James and Dreiser. Whitman's mother was a Quaker, Dreiser's a Mennonite — giving us a much clearer understanding of American radicalism, which is half Bible socialism, half sex cult.

Randolph Bourne, the son of a New Jersey minister, had also in his nature a great sex glow, and most of the portraits in his *History of a Literary Radical* were of feminists, those dry vestals of politics in the early portion of this century. Bourne was an ardent admirer of Dreiser, our sex titan, and, according to Dreiser, was never seen at table without being surrounded by, at least, two to four intelligent, erotical Venuses.

Some publisher more avid for fame than for perishable dollars would do the country and himself great honor by reprinting *Untimely Papers,* a book that is a legend — a very expensive one. Three sages, Tolstoi, Thoreau, and Bourne, are knit together by state-fear; it is astonishing that Randolph Bourne, dead at thirty-two, was as state-wise as Leo Tolstoi.

DOMESTIC MANNERS OF THE
AMERICANS

MRS. TROLLOPE, A LADY OF BREEDING from the London drawing rooms, arrived at the mouth of the Mississippi River on Christmas Day in 1827. She saw many primeval, forest settlements, bleak merchant towns, and industrial gray cities in the new republican utopia. Her book on the *Domestic Manners of the Americans* made her the object of scandalous newspaper caricatures, and tavern and curbstone guffaws. She had a clear, acerb mind and her only sin was that she had told the truth, and what is worse, what she wrote is still just.

The difference between Mrs. Trollope's *Domestic Manners* and Twain's *Life on the Mississippi* is that the lady judged what she saw. Twain saw better, but had not a moral faculty to value the spectacle. Twain wrote some passages on Mrs. Trollope's famous but reviled book in his *Life on the Mississippi*, acknowledging her understanding and probity; but either his wife Livia, or Twain, or the publisher excised his remarks. The wives of American authors have been comfort-and-prudence Ophelias, and the ruin of Twain, as well as Stephen Crane, Hamlin Garland, and Herman

87]

Melville. Perhaps Thoreau remained unwived for the best of American reasons.

Mrs. Trollope was a middle-class female burgher rather than an incendiary feminist. She had a husband, was the mother of the celebrated novelist Anthony Trollope, and had come to the United States to build a great merchandising emporium in Cincinnati. Her views were much too stable and bourgeois to be compared with those of some of our indigenous sirens who had helped build heterodoxical colonies like Oneida, the Shaker colony at Mount Lebanon, Brook Farm, the Fruitlands, and New Harmony in Indiana. It is, anyway, very startling to see just what Mrs. Trollope wrote that so vexed journalists, hotelkeepers, senators, barristers, and the sovereign pulpit.

Mrs. Trollope, on board the steamboat *Belvedere*, the gaudy stagecoach of the rivers, traveled for at least a thousand miles on the dirty, aboriginal waters which had once been named "Concepcion" by the priest Marquette in honor of the Virgin Mary. She observed the clumps of livid woodcutters' huts, the swamps, the blank cliffs of corrupt, invidious vegetation along the banks relieved by some palmettos, canebrakes, red peppers, and the tender blooming orange at Natchez and New Orleans. Twain too has left a record of these heartbreak mud-settlements brewed in the slime of Tartarus, and named after old Mediterranean Egyptian towns, Cairo, Memphis, Alexandria. Mrs. Trollope had heard some elysian rumors regarding Natchez, and sweet, hilly Memphis, fragrant with pawpaw and fruits, but found instead rheumy, malarial towns, hemmed in on all sides by savage forests. The American had been slain by the implacable sequence of demented trees, bogs, and rivers that hissed among the stones. She visited her friend, Frances Wright, and admired her flinty zeal at the Nashoba Plantation which she had established for fifteen suffering Africans; but after a few days of heavy, seedy rains and a roofless bedroom, Mrs. Trollope left.

There was Cincinnati, situated on a rugged bluff, where she had looked for artistic salons, theaters, and the epigrams of a Sheridan or a North American Swift or Pope. She had discovered, instead a rough, barren

Sparta of some twenty thousand inhabitants, where there was neither poverty nor wealth, nor civilized entertainments. There were low taxes, and herds of filthy pigs in the main thoroughfare. At the family hotel table d'hote sixty to seventy men stuffed their desperado gullets in grum, funerary silence, and then hurried away to the paper mills or to a wizened farm of a few cows, pigs, maize, and poultry, while their wives remained at home over their kettles and republican mush. The pastimes were tall stories, hawking, spitting, and pioneer tobacco-chewing. It was the age of the brass cuspidor, and no thriving public place in Kansas City, Wichita, or Joplin was without its Greekish amphora, into which rounders, crimps, and dice-coggers expectorated as a recreation.

What oppressed Mrs. Trollope most was North American tedium; Henry James remarked that amusements were almost confined to the church pew. There was homicidal logic in the unrelenting sameness of the forest, the dreary knot of hills without flowers, save some atoning pennyroll herbs, and the usual dementia thickets and underbrush.

It was said that Mrs. Trollope had the lynx optics of the female rather than the large, prodigal views of the male traveler. It was a gross falsehood. Edgar Howe's book, *The Story of a Country Town*, is a terrible American epitaph, and Hamlin Garland's Dakota farms are a record of the solitude of these aboriginal plebeians.

Mrs. Trollope was taken aback by what she felt was specious independence in the American; a nearby cottager would ask for the loan of milk, eggs, or cheese, but when they were offered free, the borrower was startled and would never say thank you. It is a common national fault; what Bolingbroke said, "Thanks, forevermore the exchequer of the poor," is more difficult for the American to heave out of his mouth than for Cordelia to utter her affections for her father, Lear.

Mrs. Trollope also found revivalism abhorrent, and shaking, quaking, and other teeming convulsions more erotical than holy. What she failed to perceive was that many of our most provincial foibles were bequeathed to the Americans by the mother country. The quaking puritans had their origin in England; the Shakers were founded by Mother Ann Lee, an illiterate cultist from London; Robert Dale Owen, who died a spiritualist and who had founded the socialist and free-thought colony at New Harmony, Indiana, was a Manchester manufacturer. Outside of London, England was provincial, and most of the Englanders lived by the "middens and the piggeries." Maybe they had more subdued manners, for it takes a long time for people to learn when and when not to spit, cough, and sneeze. As late as Chesterfield's time, this lord had advised his son that a gentleman should neither play the fiddle nor look into his handkerchief after he blew his nose. The picaresque novels of England should have been a great republican school for Mrs. Trollope. Fielding's English country squires had the natural habits of a stable peasant, or of an unbowdlerized Falstaff.

We are a stygian silent people, and it may be that we are the inheritors of the obituary forest and the great bison tracts of the Platte. We are bleached and spectral Redmen still looking for our inceptions. The big, paranoiac cities have made us more solitary and rude, and we produce remarkably pretty women who walk with funerals in their faces. What is astounding is that our faults are not newborn, but go back to the homestead — the wild alkali towns of Bierce, Twain, and Stephen Crane. Manners that time should have made hospitable and domestic have already decayed and are tumored. We came into a vast heritage of earth and energy, but the land and the people are still unsettled. How will the American rediscover his Pike's Peak, his Rocky Mountain strength, his origins, now buried with the Indian and the fossil mammoths? Mrs. Trollope was not a sibyl, a drawing-room Cassandra; she was very intelligent, and only told those truths that have come from our own indigenous seers whom we have canonized, but not heeded.

OUR VANISHING COOPERATIVE COLONIES

SUNSET HAS FALLEN upon American letters, though it is less than a hundred years ago that we had a meadowy, daybreak verse and essay. It looked as though we were on the verge of some unusual sunrise; the land was pasture; Thoreau's *Walden* was a woodland lesson and prayer in how to live without wasting the human spirit. Whitman was like a large, sacred heifer, lowing over the heads of the communal sons and daughters of these states. We were an agrarian people, smelling of the harvest and orchard and of good, savory cattle stalled and colonized together. Now we are becoming city untouchables, and manufacturers are making enormous profits out of deodorants and mouthwashes which are supposed to relieve people of real or imaginary odors. Having almost any kind of smell that may come from wine or food or toilet is a miserable tabu, and a sign of how separated we are. I think we are more afraid of being near each other than committing some dark vice.

How quickly people make a cult of their fears. Some call being alone good health, but that is just being complex and froward. The truth is, company is very easing and ablutional, and after being with people we feel better and cleaner than after soap and a bath. Do we have to be very wise to know that we are ailing? We are afraid to speak plainly, without canting clothes, and admit that many of us are suffering more from the pangs of loneliness than anything else. The world we live in does not belong to us, and it has made us wild, city waifs. Yet it is unjust to live alone, because people who live by themselves become lawless, brooding bipeds. Melville said that the separate man was the "vulture of himself," and I believe that icy solitude killed Melville as an author.

Trade, no less than American verse, is feral and hermetic and devious. What is cold and inhuman has seeped down into the market, the store, and into poetry. The grubbiest vendor drops a coin into the customer's hand without touching him. We have a brand-new sanitary goddess of trade, Hygeia. Are we cowering before touch? Do we really want to be that clean? Maybe there is skulking greed in this new, repulsive shopkeeping deity. Shake a man's hand, or smile, and it is harder to be a conscienceless cheat. The grum, coffin faces behind counters are like Pilate who was always washing his hands. The touchless store- and verse-men are driving us back into dreams and into suprahuman regions where they cannot touch us at all! We are too ashamed to admit this, and think we are complex. We are so clever that we are fast dying from it.

Engineers, mechanics, college professors, we are no longer a manual people. Something has happened to our hands. The automobile has rendered them loveless, and now they skulk in our pockets and purses like guilt. The auto-man is handless and legless; he doesn't see or walk, and yet he is always going someplace, and he is crazy to view people. The auto-man is BIG, and he is for BULK. There is the story of the American merchant in Taxco, Mexico. He had a sort of Indian trader's post in that city, which looked like some old Greek or Italian travelogue town through whose streets wandered mules, horses, and goats. An Indian from the hills showed the American trader a chair he had made. The American thought it was a fine, handmade chair, and he asked him how much he wanted for it. The Indian replied: "You can have the chair for ten pesos." The Ameri-

[92

can said, "How much would twenty chairs like that cost me?" The Indian thought a while and answered: "That would be twelve pesos for each chair." The startled American retorted: "Why do I have to pay twelve pesos a chair for an order of twenty, when you just said I could have one chair for ten pesos?" The Indian said, "Think how boring it would be to have to make the same chair twenty times."

Making things knits people together; hands that are slow and patient are wise and loving and companionable. Maybe all our trouble with wedlock now goes back to hands; that is what is wrong with the modern city, the desolate, single roomer, male and female, with an angora or boxer for companion. It is said that thievery, cheating, adultery, divorce, or being lonely were almost unknown in the Mayan towns. In the Indian handicraft hamlets wedlock thrived, but in our North American iron cities divorce flourishes, and what we call monogamy is having one wife at a time. Mayans made plum, maize, and bread towns; these were granary settlements like farmland Kansas or Ohio, where the home was important. Today it is the street rather than the house that is social and where persons meet, and the street is no good for marriage or trust or love. When the street dominates the nation, the artisan and the house die. The old Egyptians used to take the shoes of their wives with them when they went to business so that their wives could not go into the street and be unfaithful. The ancient books that we still love most are house and marriage songs, like the Book of Ruth in which Ruth tells Boaz that she wants to be his bride by lying at his feet on the corn-heap. Wedlock, and artisanship, and death are a family ritual. We are terribly afraid of death or of dying alone, in a hotel room, unwept and unkissed. It is hard to believe that Jacob, expiring on the threshing floor at Atad, surrounded by his sons, regarded his fate as severe. When the old people of a Mayan village got tired of being alive or did not want to wait to be senile or useless, they lay down in their hammocks and died.

We must get away from size, being big, just because it is much better hygiene to be affectionate, or what Whitman called adhesive. Once there were small, communal cooperatives in America. Some Americans in the nineteenth century said this was living in community and others that it was being our brother's keeper. There were little human and economic associations in nineteenth-century America, like the Oneidans, Shakers, Mennonites, Rappites, and Amish, Amana, and Aurora colonies. About eighty utopian colonies or settlements flourished in the United States. Every one with human feeling is a utopian, whether he is a garment worker or a Leo Tolstoi. The cooperative ideal is not merely a bookish conception. William Morris, the English socialist who did beautiful printing on a handpress, translated Homer, and was a lover of the old chair, table, and household crafts, thought that all that was needed for a golden age of letters was a race of women with tender ankles and thick wheaten sheaves of hair.

We have witnessed the dying out of the crafts, for we live in mechanical apartments surrounded by loveless chairs, sofas, carpets which have no relation to the heart or the fingers. Thoreau said we reason from our hands to our heads. There is much babble about children and the family, though the intellectuals' ideal appears to be one child or a sterile marriage. Julius Caesar, visiting an Asiatic city, and seeing the matrons caressing dogs and monkeys, said these women must be barren.

There are so many rascal ironies that result from trade, and from such idols as education and comfort. We are wild to have ancient origins and go mad for antiques, though most of Washington Square, where Henry James, Dreiser, and Sherwood Anderson once lived, has been destroyed by New York University.

Business has despoiled the nation of its landmarks, or made a clownish mischief of them. In Salem, Massachusetts, opposite the Lydia Pinkham Foundation, is the Nathaniel Hawthorne garage. On Grove Street in Manhattan's Greenwich Village, where Thomas Paine wrote *The Crisis*, is a cafe by that name. There is not even a plaque or any other mark on the Twenty-sixth Street dwelling where Herman Melville wrote some of his books.

Once we were a nation of cabinetmakers, farmers, pewterers, silversmiths, potters, and lived in community. Paul Revere, celebrated in stupid textbooks for the ride to Concord, though he never got there, was a remarkable silversmith. Lincoln's father made spinning wheels, and Stephen Douglas began as a cabinetmaker. Andrew Johnson, so maligned in public-school books, was an honest, illiterate apprentice tailor at fourteen. It was the custom of the master tailor to hire somebody to read to the men in the shop while they sewed, and in this way Johnson commenced his learning.

Colonial arts were often a family matter; there were the ten pewtering Danforths and the twelve silvering Moultons who recall the twenty-two J. S. Bach children of music. The community idea and artisanship went together. William Savory, a Quaker, and John Goddard of the same sect made some of the finest Chippendale furniture. There was Henry William Stiegel, the most famous glassworker in colonial America. Stiegel had communal visions; he built the town of Manheim in Pennsylvania, and populated it with glassworkers from Sweden, Switzerland, and Lorraine. Stiegel was a sort of manorial patrician; he was so kind to his Manheim townsmen that he was sent to a debtor's prison. Stiegel glass is very rare today, and very expensive, though Stiegel himself spent his latter days at menial jobs, and no one even knows where he is buried.

The colonial artisans, who built pottery kilns, made stoves and glass, were our first bohemians; they were generally in debt and a little illicit. Richard Graves, one of the earliest pewterers, settled in Salem around 1635. Graves had an illegal Falstaff nature, liking whisky, scandal, and shuffleboard, a game reckoned a vice among the puritans. He was fined and whipped for having kissed Goody Gent twice. Pewtermakers were known as "sadware men," sad meaning heavy, and that seems very right for men who had jolly wise hands so apt with pewter or drink or women or glass. Like Falstaff they were sad and heavy at the end, when they were no longer artisans, and were out of pocket. John Christopher Heyne's pewter has virtually disappeared, for so much of that metal was melted down for bullets for the Revolutionary War. His pieces are museum relics today — no more than a half dozen are known to be his. In the last war the British government took most of the people's pewter for ammunition and cannon.

It is not an unrelated fact that the sects thrived when the artisan was in the land. The visionaries of Aurora, and the Shakers, and the Amish were unlettered craftsmen with acute minds. George Rapp, founder of the colony at Economy, Pennsylvania, was a vine-dresser. The Aurorans, who went out to Oregon in covered wagons, were tanners, blacksmiths, cobblers, tailors, and bakers. The Amish and Moravians and Mennonites, known as Pennsylvania Dutch, extremely intelligent land-peasants, could hardly read or write. The Shakers — whose remarkable founder was Mother Ann Lee who had no schooling at all — made settles, chairs, doughchests, ovens that are precious relics. The people in communal Oneida, New York, were famous for their steel traps and silverware.

The Amish Bible illiterates, coming from Germany, Switzerland, New England, and the Tennessee mountains, all had Old and New Testament names — Amos, Lot, Sarah, Martha. The name was very important in the old America; good, honest cheese came from a reliable family, and so did a fine wife. The exiled Jews returning to Jerusalem were not allowed to be a singer or even a porter unless their names, which were proofs of the trades of their families, were in the Judaic Register.

In the nineteenth century many people fled from the yoke of the flesh, living as celibates, like the Shakers or Rappites, or like Bachelor Whitman, the sex poet, or else sought brotherhood and community by being erotical. Henry Ward Beecher at Plymouth Church in Brooklyn was delivering hot, amative sermons, some of which sound like lines out of Whitman's *Leaves of Grass*. Whitman was a friend of Beecher, who was also an intimate of Victoria Woodhull, one of the first feminists and erotical sirens. This was the heyday of the vascular amative Adam and the free-loving Eve. John Humphrey Noyes, the Oneida Community leader, had written his Battle-Axe Letter, a manifesto on sex. Beecher himself, preaching the gospel of the flesh to his congregation, had swayed so many women that his amours became known as the Great Brooklyn Scandal.

The sects were either a Garden of Eden for freelovers or a commune of the most dour ascetics. The Amana were a marrying people, though not particularly jocular, for matrimony was not considered a meritorious act. Their leader, Barbara Heynemann, had been rebuked because she had a

[96

carnal eye for one of the Amana brothers, whom she later wedded. One of the ironies of nineteenth-century America is that the name of this colony was taken from the sensual song of Solomon, "Come with me from Lebanon, my spouse . . . look from the top of Amana." Lebanon, the name of the place in New York where the celibate Shakers dwelt, is a place for cedars, the marriage-house, and the amorous pillow. There is another paradox: the ascetic Shakers go back to revolutionary days, and lasted longer than any other primitive communistic sect in the United States.

The Amana settlement at Iowa was established in 1865 on twenty-five thousand acres of land upon which were erected barns, mills, and shoe-making, carpenter, and tailor shops. They held their goods in common as did most of the sects who practiced religious communism. The Shakers derived their communistic tenets from the Essenes who lived in Judea in small communal villages before Christ.

In the earliest Amana settlements each family had a brick or frame house, although they ate at a common table. Their laws have a strong Marxist flavor, although their faith is based on the words of Luke in Acts: "And all that believe were together, and had all things in common . . . distribution was made unto every one according as he had need." Most present-day communists are unmindful of Marx's debt to Paul and Luke.

The Amana folk baked excellent bread, made fine beer which they drank in moderation at summer meals, and like the Shakers regarded ornaments as the vanity of the world. The Amana, Rappite, and Shaker garb was homespun, and in the marrying colonies there were no divorces or separations, no painted Jezebels or whoring Rahabs. The frugal Amana apron, the wide, rough, peasant skirt, may not entice the modern man who, as D. H. Lawrence remarked, is more interested in the underclothing of women than in herself. One cannot help wondering about modern women, wearing their hair loose over their shoulders, and looking as though they were prepared not so much for the street as for their bedrites.

The church at Amana, like that of the Amish, Moravians, and Quakers, had no steeple, the brethren no paid clergyman. Most of the meetings were held in barns or sheds as among the Pennsylvania-Dutch Amish.

Some may regard these communal settlers as bitingly spartan, but though they were industrious, they made no cult of work, and they believed as Tolstoi did that work in itself is no more of a virtue than voiding or eating. Also like Tolstoi, they believed literally in the Sermon on the Mount. They were nonresisters and though they were opposed to slavery they took no part in the Civil War. With the exception of the socialistic settlement at New Harmony, whose leader was Robert Owen, the Manchester, England, manufacturer, drunkenness or debauchery was unknown. No jails or police or almshouses existed in any of these communities. At Oneida Community the goods, as well as the wives, were held in common; the vulgar cartoonists and philisters from newspapers who visited the community, expecting to find profligate Herods and Salomes, viewed with amazement the vineyards, bakeshops, tanneries, and the cedar and fir houses of marriage.

Except at Oneida Brook Farm (established by George Ripley, a friend of Emerson), and Fruitlands (a Pythagorean vegetable colony guided by Bronson Alcott), education was scorned. It was confined to the three R's, and to the Bible, being together, and to telling the truth. The ancient Medes taught their children how to ride, shoot, and tell the truth. At present we send millions of young persons to expensive colleges, and they are not taught to be direct or loving, or instructed in even the barest rudiments of courtesy. A Shaker could build a marvelous Dutch oven, and though he did not know who Thomas Campion was, his word was the pledge of the angels and the perdition of Lucifer.

The Fruitlanders were Yankee Pythagoreans, borrowed their tenets from the ancient sect at Crotona, Italy. The Fruitland people avoided carnal meats which they believed yielded beast dreams. They said that vegetables irrigated the soul and purged men of caitiff thoughts.

The Americans have always been food, sex, and spirit revivalists. John Noyes converted Pauline scripture into a sexual sacrament, saying that "He that doubteth is damned if he eat." None at Oneida who partook of this meal broke the faith. Noyes also wrote of the relation of the sexes in the Kingdom of Heaven. He was the first to advocate eugenics and birth control, which he called stirpiculture, for which Shaw gave him much credit. Humphrey Noyes was later to be reckoned among the Fabian saints. Sexual communism, which was an orderly ritual at Oneida, was practiced more erratically by Victoria Woodhull. Abner Kneeland, also among the nineteenth-century sex and vision shakers, founded a contraceptive colony which he called Salubria.

Many of our militant atheists have concluded their lives as clairvoyants and spiritualists. Owen of the socialist New Harmony Movement died a spiritualist. The biographer of Josiah Warren, called the father of American anarchism, was ashamed to reveal to his readers that Warren had also ended his days in the same way. On Dreiser's bookshelf in his room at the Eleventh Street Rhinelander apartments I saw William James's *The Immortality of the Soul*. James was interested in extramundane ecstasies, and Dreiser was always more than half a Christian Scientist. He went out to die in Los Angeles, the big swami-theosophy town for enema mystagogues and Seventh Day Adventist Pythagoreans who practice upper and lower colonic irrigations.

The community zealots were among the first pioneer settlers in the wilderness; the families settled Bethel, Missouri, when it was as feral as the father of waters which the priest Marquette sailed down in a canoe, marveling at the deer, the elk, the dogwood, and the prehistoric paintings on the cliffs. The Bethel colonists, seeking the Oregon apple valley as an Eden for a new commune, built covered wagons and traveled two thousand miles through the Platte where the bison, woolly cattle, ran in thick droves, and over the Rockies and Blue Mountains. Many caravans of white men had been destroyed by hostile Indians, but no harm came to these people who met the Pawnee with shirts, food, and kind faces. At Aurora, Oregon, they started their little utopia — consisting of orchards, woolen and flour mills, a distillery, a school, an ascetic white church — and prospered. Their leader was Dr. Keil, and the saintly character of Bethel and Aurora was Helen Giesy, who broke her troth with John Roebling, who had the genius to build the Brooklyn Bridge but lacked the simple, communal gospel. Related to the remarkable Giesy family of Aurora were the famous Sutro family whose name today is a part of the hills, ledges, and sea of San Francisco.

There have been modern experiments in cooperatives, such as the now defunct Black Mountain College and the MacDowell colony. The students of Black Mountain built a library, simple monkish study cells, and the dwelling places under the guidance of Neutra and Buckminster Fuller. Black Mountain had marvelous handlooms where students reproduced pre-Columbian blankets and rugs. Their former rector and one of the founders of the college was Josef Albers, an Alsatian. Albers is a celebrated abstractionist painter. The MacDowell colony for musicians, writers, and artists was started by the widow of Edward MacDowell, American composer. I knew her in her nineties when she was blind. Earlier she had been a slight, sinewy New Englander with a muscular Elizabethan laugh. She used to drive a pair of horses and carriage with battle ardor. The MacDowell colony is nine hundred acres of land abounding in enchanting studios and homes, lying in the Berkshire hills at Peterboro, New Hampshire. The colony was at first supported by money Mrs. MacDowell earned from her piano concerts, and many persons, including Edwin Arlington Robinson and Elinor Wylie, owed a fecund summer's writing to that blunt sibyl of the muses. Years ago I asked this lady why she had given so much of her life to maintain a commune for so many mediocre artists. She said that if more than twenty-five per cent of the guests were geniuses the entire colony would be disrupted. Dear, good lady, she need no longer worry about such a debacle, for what Whitman called the divine average, but which is just average, now rules.

One of the weaknesses in the cooperative is that it has never been sufficiently leavened by the imagination. This is a quick-silver faculty, and likely to be a cause of worry to any collective settlement. Nathaniel Hawthorne found his sojourn at Brook Farm very unreplenishing, for he said that after working all day for a year with manure-composts all that he was able to produce was a farmer's almanac. Codman, in his book on the Brook Farmers, had such impecunious perceptions as to remark that a charming writer of romances by the name of Henry David Thoreau had resided at

[100

Brook Farm for six months. Dana, who wrote *Two Years before the Mast*, and Margaret Fuller, whom Hawthorne referred to in his *Blithedale Romance,* the only interesting book written by an author who lived in one of these settlements, as a she-Briareus, had also been there. Channing, Thoreau's biographer, was a resident. The Brook Farmers derived their ideas from Charles Fourier. Bronson Alcott's Fruitlanders were militant vegetarians, but were said to be carnivores whenever they had the occasion to leave their peas-and-carrots commune.

It is very easy, and even slothful and smirking, to write of the failures of these many brotherhood cooperative societies. Everything ultimately fails, for we die, and that is either the penultimate failure or our most enigmatical achievement. The gospel of being together which these people practiced is perhaps the most noble effort the American has made. Men, who, as Aristotle said, are the forlorn, featherless bipeds, must live in community or hate each other. Most cooperatives have expired, and today Oneida silver or Shaker salt are no more than trademarks. There are a few remnant Shaker families at New Lebanon, which in the Bible is the lady of the mountain, or the tender Shulamite. The Shakers abstained from marriage. They did not pretend this was easy, but they feared marriage more than many of us love it, and like the prophet Hosea, betrayed by the world and his wife Gomer, turned to Israel and to Zion as the Bride.

The Amish still persist in Lancaster, Pennsylvania, and elsewhere in the country. They shun automobiles, radios, movies, and though they are farmers, they still use the horse which dungs the furrow. These prohibitions may seem droll to many, but there is great wisdom in bucolic ideals. The Luddites in England, whom Byron and Shelley celebrated in poems, broke the machines with their hands.

Tolstoi had the greatest distrust of progress, which he called a superstition. Machinery is a baleful sign of tedium, inertia, and desolation. When Gorki came to this country and was taken to Coney Island he said the Americans must be a mournful people to seek their entertainments in mechanical amusements.

The great idol, Baal, is the new, and we have little time to go back to our origins because we are always hankering after novelities in words, poetry, and pastimes. A dozen years ago, Leon Kramer, a bookdealer with perhaps more knowledge than anybody else about early American communities, sold a wonderful collection of such invaluable material to the University at Rotterdam. Since then there has been a reawakened interest in these sects, and a number of new books on them has been published. There are the *Yankee Saint,* about John Humphrey Noyes, by Allerton Parker, worldly but valuable, and a volume lately done on the Moravians, the Mennonites, and the Amish by Keels, written with a journalistic and academic simper. There are a volume written with feeling on Bethel and Aurora by Robert J. Hendrick, and John Humphrey Noyes' *History of American Socialisms,* a real curiosity. Charles Nordhoff published a very useful book on these sects in 1875. The most piercing remarks about any of these loving sons and daughters of our new Galilee are in Leo Tolstoi's letters concerning the Russian Dukhobors, nonresisters who went to Canada, and one of whose leaders is the daughter of Tolstoi. Tolstoi never smirked at the simple, naive heart, which has far more intelligence than the mind. Tolstoi, himself — always valiantly fighting against those evils he believed monstered people, good clothes, meat, sex, ambition, fame, and who was as flesh-yoked as St. Paul or St. Augustine — tells how the Czar sent the fierce cossacks to whip and tame the humble Dukhobors who refused to go into the army. In the end the cossacks who punished their victims with rifle-butts, and who received from their victims the most gentle words about the Sermon on the Mount, and not doing violence to those that harm us, had to be transported elsewhere because they had become nonresisting Dukhobors.

Truth and trust prevail better in small places, like Judea, Attica, the Nile towns, or the rural Midwest. We see how human confidence has vanished with the bitterness of Herman Melville's novel in which he has the trimmer make the only wise remarks about trust and charity. Those who have no appetite for the reading of Kropotkin or Randolph Bourne or the nineteenth-century Nazarene rebels, can establish small human cooperatives where the sons and daughters of a new Zion may consider the lilies.

Aristotle has said that men who live alone are either wild beasts or gods, but there are so many of the former and maybe none of the latter, that it is better to be men and women together.

People continue to think about progress. A few years ago there was an epidemic in an Indian settlement outside of Santa Fe in which many children perished. Officials of the American government suggested that doctors be sent into the adobe Indian colony to take care of the sick, but the Indians refused, saying, "First comes the doctor, then the Ford and the machines, and after that the Indian disappears." The Indians of the southwest have the most tender regard for their wives and children, but they think they are more civilized than we are. Is the solitary American superior to the communal Indian?

FLORENTINE CODEX

FATHER BERNARDINO DE SAHAGUN, a Franciscan monk of Mexico, started his *Florentine Codex*, a work on the Aztecs, in Tepeopulco in the sixteenth century. He had attended the famous university at Salamanca where the modern, passionate visionary and philosopher Miguel de Unamuno taught in our own time. Sahagun's Mexican history, in twelve books, consisted chiefly of hieroglyphs drawn by the Indians, and their interpretation in Aztec. The original Mexican codex was trilingual: Nahuatl (Mexican), Spanish, and Latin. The famous Fanny Bandelier translation is from the Spanish of Bustamante, but the *Florentine Codex* is a literal translation from the Aztec, containing two of the twelve books.

Sahagun, unlike Torquemada and the Bishop Diego de Landa, was a soft-going man, with abundant affections for the Indians whom he taught in New Spain. He had the strongest abhorrence of the Indian idols and human sacrifice. On one occasion he climbed to the almost inaccessible peaks of two volcanoes, Iztaccihuatl and Popocatepetl, to find the craters where the Indians sacrificed children, captives, and women to appease their fierce gods. At another time, learning that there was a stone idol hidden in a spring of sweet water, he went down into the pool and erected in the place of the Aztec image a cross. Diego de Landa, though he wrote some marvelous matter on the Mayans of Yucatan, so detested their man-eating practices that he burnt all their writings and glyphs: Father Sahagun simply observed them.

The two volumes of the *Florentine Codex* are about the gods, the ancient ceremonies, and the calendar. The Aztec calendar was more accurate than the Julian or Gregorian. They had eighteen months in their year, each month containing twenty days, and, in addition, five extra days which were known as the barren days.

Their vows and penances were as important as their festivals. When there was drought, the priests of the Tlalocs fasted so that the rains would come. During the rain festival, which took place in the sixteenth month, they made anthropomorphic images of their mountains, and set in the heads teeth of squash seeds and eyes of beans.

The old Aztec tongue was an extremely strong language ruled by the cactus, the eagle, the nettles and flowers of the Sierras. It would reinvigorate American English to include Mexican Indian words and symbols. These fierce and astonishing peoples have been the lodestar of a number of American figures — the historian William Prescott, Hart Crane and William Carlos Williams, the poets, Ambrose Bierce, the short-story writer, and the late Haniel Long, author of that sweet chapbook, *The Power within Us,* the American fable of Cabeza de Vaca.

The twelve books cost their author much pain and humbling, for it is a miracle that these precious histories ever came to public knowledge. His superior, a monk of far less probity and learning than Sahagun, refused to let him have any copyists to rewrite the annals, saying that such an expense violated the Franciscan vows of poverty. Sahagun had labored over the rites, gods, and songs of the Aztecs until his hand was too old and feckless to hold a pen. Then the superior had the twelve books dispersed so that they could be scrutinized by other priests in different Mexican cloisters. That the simple ascetic Franciscan, who appears to have had only two unworldly desires, to believe and to know, should have been the object of human envy would be an enigma if we did not know greedy human flesh.

The religion of the Aztec will repel many subtle readers; it will not so much ravel the conscience as the imagination, for people are more upset by blood than morally wounded by its presence. The Mexican gods are figures of war, and gore, and evil, and they are in part reptile, bird, ocelot, and vulture. The Aztec religion is in many ways a gospel for the lion, the osprey, the cormorant, rather than a faith for the gentler peoples who inhabit the four directions of the world; yet there are no men anywhere who have not blood that does not boil or raven as the beast. It is true the Aztecs were adepts in special vices, that their greatest ecstasies were had from flaying, flailing, and eating people, and that all their festivals were generally consummated by anthropophagous rites. Still, they had laws and ceremonies regarding drunkenness, chasity, adultery, stealing, and perjury, which we observe with less zeal than the sluggard, or the pismire. The most pedestrian stealth was punished by slavery. Adultery was a great crime, and could be punished by death. The North American Indians — inferior to the Aztec in art and manual civilities such as weaving, featherwork, the growing of maize, the singing of psalms to flowers and honey and hemp — also viewed adultery with gravity. It is told that the malefactor could not be slain unless the husband found him in his consort's bed, which then required much more vigilance than at present. Lying was particularly offensive to the Aztec and the Inca, whereas today it is the habit of all countries to set up special liar departments.

The Aztecs had a pious regard for crafts, plants, maize, copal or incense, wine, pulque, reeds, papyrus; they wrote with the reed, and the Aztecan idols, astounding pieces of sculpture, were clothed in paper, in quetzal feathers intricately woven, and in cotton upon which were marvelously wrought stags, monkeys, deer, and signs for wind, rain, and misfortune. The ancient Mexican made rush seats out of the same kind of reed he wrote with.

Custom is the king of man, said Pindar the Greek poet. What then is politics but the study of human habits? The tribal Mexican gods of maize, tamale, amaranth seeds, and the stone and cactus idols teach us more about politics, which is the study of manners, raiment, food, marriage, work, than the study of money which has become the main fetish of modern nations. Money, a species of senilia, was not used by the Incas, or the Aztecs who bartered cocoa for labor and food and clothes. This was a great wisdom, for money is the most terrible serpent and killer; it tears the festivals, the flowers, the dance, and the heart out of people. There is a strange and mighty race of people called the Americans who are rapidly becoming the coldest in the world because of this cruel, maneating idol, lucre, which did not exist among the cruder and less civil Aztecs.

BEYOND THE PILLARS OF HERCULES

THE MATERIALS OF THE INDIAN MANUSCRIPTS show remarkable culture; the Aztecan papyrus was of the fabric of the agave
whose maguey leaves were employed as thatch for the roofs of the houses
and as indigenous food and drink. The Mexican idolaters built Tenoch-
titlan, meaning cactus on a stone, which is modern Mexico City. Their
primitive language, their gods, and their raiment reveal an understanding
often far in advance of our own civilization; it is told that the Indians Co-
lumbus took as vassals and friends had devils embroidered on their dresses
which bore the likeness of owls, and that they called the evil spirits rational
owls, which indicates more wisdom than the Hegelian bird of Minerva.

The Americas, new savage earth, which breed natural, mineraled cruel-
ties as well as recondite courtesies; Indian morals are no less astounding
than those of the Spanish conquistadores who came in sixteenth-century
wood caravels with white and blue sails and banners raised in homage
to Our Lady. It cannot be asserted that the most cultivated natures from
Christian Madrid or Barcelona were more urbane than the Indian pagans

who sometimes ate people, a very common practice everywhere, though polite nations have always marveled at it. Many other customs, more congenial and domestic, are interred in archives or in unread, mummified books. It is told that Montezuma's men kissed the earth and fumigated Cortes and his soldiers "with incense brought in braziers of pottery."

The Aztecans have an idol, Cihuacoatl, which means woman and serpent, and she is the mother of mankind. The same word is applied to justice and law, and this is wise scripture, for it shows a slight regard for the ratiocinative faculty, and an extraordinary understanding of customs.

With these words, and being myself no idolater, having the most humble veneration of God, and paying respect to the Lady Mary, let me recount a moiety of the history of Florida as it is related by the mestizo, half European and half Inca, Garcilaso de la Vega.* He who is both European and American can comprehend what is barbaric and what is domestic, for together they are man, who, as Pascal said, is part angel and part beast.

The Florida conquest is a fable of primeval ground. The author of *The Florida* was the issue of a Peruvian Inca princess and a soldier of Emperor Carlos the Fifth of Spain. Printed in Madrid in 1605, the book of the Inca prince is an account of the passion play of gold and piety in the New Indies. It is also a record of the many miseries of the conquistadores who attempted to convert the sun and moon infidels of the Americas, who were as immune to the cross as the other heathen demons, the boreal rivers, the maize, the mountains, the cliffs, and the bogs. The conquerors were alchemic discoverers with a metaphysical avarice, for they coveted everything — the yellow, edenic ore, the people, and their aboriginal hemisphere. But they were to fail, for though they came in the name of the Apostle Santiago, the New Indies, like the new elements, was a circean drug which translated the Europeans into an indigenous race of Christian savages.

Hernando de Soto was the admiral and leader of the armada which contained 950 Spaniards, including 12 friars, 250 horses, and some sows for breeding purposes; he died in 1542, three years after landing in Florida,

* Translated by John and Jeanette Varner, Austin, University of Texas Press, 1951.

of a fever said to be sorrow. His remains were deposited in the hollow of an oak which was lowered into the Mississippi. Other discoverers who came to New Spain lost their reason and expired. It may be surmised that they sinned against locality, a god to the Indian caciques who bore the names of the rivers, the hills, or forests where they abode. The holy ground possesses the Indians, and though there was terrible hostility between one Indian settlement and another, the victors decapitating their enemies and enslaving their wives and children, they seldom took each other's land.

The Spanish discoverers gave pious homage to the new provinces. Juan Ponce de Leon, driven upon a coast near Cuba on the day of the Feast of the Resurrection, called the region Florida, which means the coming up of flowers. The vessels in De Soto's armada bore the names of saints, and the inlets and coves are memorials of their reverence and misfortunes. The Bay of the Holy Spirit and the River of Discords are the sighs of sacred geographers. They wanted to own the Tierra Nueva and for their evil desires, place was translated into a nemesis instead of an angel, and most of them perished or were deprived of their wits.

The Governor and Captain General of the Kingdom of Florida was a most civil nature, giving the Indian *curaca* (chief, governor) silks, mirrors, and shirts, and embracing him with the greatest affection. He also commanded his cavalry to ride as a martial battalion, because the natives thought the horse and man were a single beast. The curaca bowed low, kissing the hands of Adelantado de Soto, and his Indians came with maize, grapes, dried prunes, fish, and marten furs smelling of musk, while his warriors hid in the forests or near lagoons, their bows and arrows covered by grass.

The Floridians were tall, more than two yards in length. The men had handsome, feral countenances, and wore just enough chamois cloth to conceal their haunches and shameful parts. Their bows, made of oak, were as hard to draw as the one which Odysseus had the strength to employ against the suitors of Penelope.

The coastal regions were marshy; the tumid rivers flooded as far as sixty leagues inland. The maritime soil was so sterile there were times when the Spaniards had no food save sea snails and booby birds. It is told elsewhere by Friar Diego de Landa that the Spanish soldiers ate the inside of bark, which is mellow and soft.

The Cacique Hirrihigua pursued the Spaniards relentlessly. In 1528, twelve years before Hernando De Soto had proclaimed the Kingdom of Florida a possession of the Emperor Charles the Fifth, Hirrihigua seized four Spaniards who had come to this region with Pánfilo de Narváez. He took them to the plaza of the village commanding them to run while the Indians shot arrows at them. This gave him such pleasure that he ordered his warriors to torture Juan Ortiz, an eighteen-year-old "fledgling cavalier," but his wife and three daughters beseeched the Cacique to spare him, and because of their tender entreaties, he interrupted this spectacle.

It must be admitted that Hirrihigua had received some injustices from the Spaniards who threw his mother to the dogs to be eaten; also, when the Cacique had occasion to blow his nose, he could not find it. The Elvas account reports that De Soto offered similar affronts and had the hands and noses of Indians cut off, and also that the Adelantado had the lips and chins of Indians removed, leaving their faces flat. He was said to have severed the heads of fainting couriers rather than bother "to untie the collars by which they were led." On one occasion De Soto's Spaniards seized an Indian for a guide to lead them back to the sea. After marching in a circle through woods and bogs, eating roots and grass for many days, and discovering that they had been deceived, they threatened to give the Indian to the mastiffs if he did not take them back to the sea which was only several leagues away. He promised to obey them, and after circling the forests again, and making the Spaniards endure more terrible suffering, he was given to the dogs, who devoured him.

Hernando De Soto took the greatest pains to gain the affections of the Cacique Vitachuco, who had sent many messengers to him, promising that he would command the ground and the hills to swallow the Spaniards; he had also ordered birds to drop on the conquistadores a venom which would cause them to rot. However, the Adelantado invited Vitachuco to his camp, and after the exchange of many courtesies and vows of friendship,

De Soto's men entered the Cacique's deserted village. The Indians then discharged their arrows at the Spaniards from the woods for an entire day, while others remained in a cold lagoon where the water was of such depth that while three or four Indians swam one stood on their backs so that he could shoot his arrows at the enemy. When these Indians refused to surrender they were seized by Spaniards who swam after them and dragged them ashore, after which the governor gave them mirrors and silks and sent them home. De Soto then invited the Cacique to his table, and Vitachuco, who had an enormous violent body, rose while his host was still eating, and seizing the Adelantado by the neck gave him blows over the eyes, the mouth, and nose. Then, falling upon his prone and half-dead victim, he began to mangle De Soto until the Spaniards killed the barbarian.

Traveling for days with no food except grass and the tendrils of vines, the miserable band and their captain came to Cofachiqui. After receiving them, the princess of that realm removed a long pearl necklace, the pearls of which were as "thick as hazelnuts," and gave it to the Adelantado. She then took them to her ancestral sepulchre where the dead were deposited in baskets woven of cane. There were twenty-five thousand pounds of pearls in this charnel house, a fabled fortune, but little regarded by the Spaniards because they had been pierced by copper needles and the smoke had somewhat discolored them. Hernando de Soto had instructed his soldiers to make rosaries of the pearls and to pray, but all the pearls were lost or cast away.

The Lady of Cofachiqui, a beauty with immense modesties, was asked to accompany the Adelantado who was most circumspect. The Inca held the Indian damsels in the highest regard, and doubtless they were very chaste, although it is reported that when a Spaniard was caught by several Indian women they gave him such mortal pains by seizing his genital organs that he either perished or suffered from another horrible affliction. According to the Elvas account, furnished here by the vigilant and learned translators of *The Florida*, it is related that De Soto's motive was not apparent, and that the discreet maiden Cofachiqui soon afterwards escaped with a Moor from Barbary, and two Negro slaves.

After De Soto perished in the wilderness, the rabble band, reduced to three hundred Spaniards, departed in boats that were miserable river huts, and were pursued by Indians in canoes for a thousand miles down the Mississippi. Their destination was Mexico City. When they arrived in Mexico, their countrymen received them with pity, and marveled at their sorrows, and at the barbaric moods of Hirrihigua, Vitachuco, and the giant Tascaluza. They offered the unfortunate paupers fifteen hundred golden pesos, the price of a good hunting dog, for a ragged marten fur. When they learned of the thousands of pounds of imperfect pearls that had been in the ancestral sepulchres of the Princess Cofachiqui, and which the soldiers held of so small account, their desire for more information regarding such a charnel house was most subtly kindled.

There is one other truth that should be stressed and which divulges the abstruse properties of the occident. The Spaniards that came to proselytize infidel Indian earth became themselves primitives. It would also be improper to imagine that the Spaniard had more civilized guile than the natives, for both Christians and heathens had a wondrous understanding of the feral soul of man. What occurred was not a metamorphosis of the Indian, but of the Spaniard who regarded a dog a greater table delicacy than a pheasant. It is also told that the soldiers of Cortes seared their own hurts and the wounds of their horses "with the fat of the Indian."

The religion of the Floridians is in their burial baskets, raiment, and marriage customs; but the Mayans of Yucatan and the Aztecans of Mexico have left their codices, which tell us much about American inceptions. The Mayan prophetic books are called *Chilam Balam*, and Balam is etymologically so close to Baal Peor, the Philistine and Tyrian idol, that one has to hold in leash his imagination lest he make the most wanton conjectures regarding early Phoenician migrations to America. It is enough to attempt to understand how all these native theologies seeded each other. The *Chilam Balam*, containing many chanting homilies, are annals of Mayan famines and plagues, and show a great preoccupation with time.

All the native genesis myths, the *Popol Vuh* of the Quiché Mayans, the Aztec fables, and the *Chilam Balam,* are not inferior to the Babylonian Gilgamesh epic. The Mexicans believed that the gods "created" in the water a great fish which is like a crocodile, and from this fish "they made the earth." This is much like the primitive cosmologies of Xenophanes and of Hesiod, who asserted that man was first a shark or a sea creature of mud and moisture.

The lore of the Americas is still interred, and the books on the Florida Indians, the Mayans of Yucatan, and annals left by Friar Diego de Landa, Father Sahagun, Torquemada, and so many others, are essential for an understanding of the new continents. The enigma of North American literature is to be comprehended by putting one's ear to the savage ground, for American writing is aboriginal rather than reflective or homiletical. Though Thoreau read the *Bhagavad-Gita* and the *Upanishads,* his books are wild sumach tracts, and Herman Melville chose a leviathan as his epical figure. Other writers, like Crèvecoeur or Charles Francis Adams in his chronicles of Massachusetts, show a passion for the reliquary flint arrow, demonic earth and river, and virgin woods, for the New World is not domestic or European. Such old-world scholars as Baron von Humboldt and Lord Kingsborough, who devoured his patrimony printing Mexican manuscripts, were attracted to this continent. The land beyond the Pillars of Hercules has always been myth and peril, but none could resist a New Energy.

FOR STANLEY BURNSHAW

MOBY-DICK: A HAMITIC DREAM

NOBODY CAN DECEIVE A MAN so well as he can gull himself, and I do not blame anybody else for my own folly. My thought is to spare others, although I know that there is hardly a man on earth who will take advice unless he is certain that it is positively bad. As for myself, I am not homesick for the fusty books I worshiped as a youth; I am no victim of that most scurrile of all ruses, nostalgia. Let me guard what is sacred, and raze to the ground the stupid, indolent Thebaid of my past because I know Pindar's house will yet remain. I have changed my mind about Herman Melville, for I once loved this Cyclops whose father is Oceanus.

It is natural that we should have a wizened, intellectual literature — and who would want to empty our little Hippocrene? — but it is malignant to feign that we are the new Attica of literature. When poeticules assert that Philip Freneau is a bard or that the pages of Charles Brockden Brown are not hellebore to the reader, he is establishing a republic of letters for solemn apes. How much noise is made for a drumbling poetaster or a Thersites of scatological fiction! Let a man, as Rabelais writes, "chew ordure" in twenty novels, and for such coprology he is wreathed in tamarisk as though he were a god instead of a sweeper of privies. We venerate size and bulk and the surest way to be accounted a genius is to write the same big, ignorant book many times.

Herman Melville, who died in 1891, had been interred by the currish literati. His hapless shade is now the object of the barkings of the same Cerberuses; beagles with the graveled throats always stand at the gate of Hades and bay the moon whenever they scent carrion — dead works.

Canting, stuffed praise of deceased writers is starved malice; whenever a critic tells such falsehoods about our past he shows his hunger and envy, and instead of providing us with a more opulent Parnassus, he parches the American Elysium. He carries, as Ben Jonson writes, "a commonwealth of paper in his hose."

Is it necessary to declare that there was not one erudite versifier or prose stylist in nineteenth-century America to compare with those geniuses who flourished when London was the fairest Hellas? There was no Mermaid Inn in New York where one could savor a beaker of ale with learned poets; the sepulchral Spouter Inn of New Bedford, whose proprietor is Peter Coffin, was no substitute for the coffee houses and the chocolate shops in which one might find a Will Congreve, Swift, Pope, Dryden, or Wycherley to be a whetstone for his own faculties. Dio Chrysostom said that the father of Achilles selected Phoenix to teach his son the arts of discourse. No matter how charitable we are to Hawthorne, Whitman, or to Poe, of what advantage could they be to poor, torn Herman Melville? Ruth could glean more barley in Boaz's field after it had been reaped than Melville could have culled from Poe's *Marginalia* or Whitman's *Democratic Vistas*. Boaz was far more prodigal, but kindness, the father of good thoughts, does not permeate belles-lettres in the United States.

Herman Melville was as separated from a civilized literature as the lost Atlantis was said to have been from the great peoples of the earth. Allen Tate, in his oracular poem, "The Mediterranean," has comprehended the sorrows that lie beyond the Pillars and the Sea of Darkness:

[116

What country shall we conquer, what fair land
Unman our conquest and locate our blood?
We've cracked the hemispheres with careless hand!
Now, from the Gates of Hercules we flood

Westward, westward till the barbarous brine
Whelms us to the tired land . . .

Let nobody imagine that I am unmindful of Herman Melville's scorify-
ing deprivations; he burnt in Puritan ice, but not in woman; God shrive his
shade, and may we sin less, for all flesh is error. Our best writers, Thoreau,
Whitman, Melville, Hawthorne, Emily Dickinson, and Poe, produced
frigid works: "admire and model thyself after the whale! Do thou, too,
remain warm among ice," is the admonition of a man whose sorest affliction was that his vitals froze in all latitudes. However, I am concerned with
Zeus Asklepios, the healing powers of a god-like book upon the American
polity.

There was a dearth of those masculine fiery particles in the Puritan.
Aristophanes averred: "By Jupiter, testicles are capital things." The nineteenth-century American was still the vassal of that Puritanic Beelzebub,
Cotton Mather, the father of the Christian homosexual. What else could
be the result of Thoreau's celibacy, Hawthorne's inclement identity, Whitman's ambiguous bachelordom, or Poe's and Melville's misogyny but the
contemporary Pauline invert? Not one of these unusual men could produce a seminal poem or a great confession like St. Augustine's. Born to
sin because we have genital organs, we live to confess our faults, and that
is scripture and literature.

Man is a tragic animal because he has a teleological impulse to prove
that he is reasonable though he knows he is not. Nothing can be proved,
and the need to assert that the Archangels Gabriel and Uriel exist is the
valor and cosmic energy in the human race. Agamemnon reproaches Cal-
chas for never having prophesied good fortune for him. We would have the
right to blame the universe for all our faults did not such a feeble attitude
bring us greater woes. One assails a poet who does not feign well. We expect an author whose life has been foolish, stupid, and full of misfortunes

117]

to be clever, sage, and quick in his books; otherwise poems betray us as much as life does.

The Word is the Logos, which is the domestic white Cock, and the phallus that impregnates the body and the soul. One of the heresiarchs claimed that the Logos was the offspring of Mercury, but the Word in New England literature never became flesh. What congealed works came from those savants! Style is the absolute limit of a man's character and bad writing shows a lack of love; its most malignant symptom is delay. Henry James postponed his periods as long as he could, and Melville deferred action until the last few pages of *Moby-Dick*. Of the hundred and thirty-one chapters, only the last three before the Epilogue are about the pursuit of Moby-Dick, and the *Pequod* is always in the calms. The whaling craft is similar to Zeno's paradoxical arrow, which, though hurled through space, is at rest in different places. There is no motion in this novel, without which there cannot be any positive affection or heat in the mind.

A good remark uttered in cumbersome words feebly put together is evil. Not one wise thought can be told without great energy. When the will languishes the demons are triumphant. Whatever one knows comes from the motions of the will. We know ourselves by our acts. Velleity is the principal reason for human perversity.

Sick books beget far more ailing ones just as potently as Abraham begat Isaac, and Isaac Jacob. Moreover, Melville's solitude was, in part, willful. As Sir Francis Bacon explains: "those that want friends to open themselves unto, are cannibals of their own hearts." We have been Ishmaels of letters since the republic was established, banished by society. Although poems are composed in sepulchral rooms, for writing is as private as dying, a healthful song is a hymn to the sun, and not, as Melville felt, "a dismal stave of psalmody." Seneca's advice is: "It is every man's duty to make himself profitable to mankind." But when the imagination of the writers is ill and distempered, the social corpus is also cankered. Melville's separation from the human race was as deranged as Bartleby's. Melville refers to the seafarers in the *Pequod* as *Isolatoes* who did not acknowledge "the common continent of men." Ishmael, who has a "damp, drizzly November" in his watery soul, is as boreal as the first Void and as much of a beggar in the winds as Lazarus.

Epictetus, who had all the fortitude of the Stoic, held quite a different view from the author of *Moby-Dick*: "Miserable man, is there any one that maintains himself? Only the universe does that." How many people, who have known the acute pangs of solitude, go abroad to tell everybody that their utmost felicity is in being absolutely alone, a rapture easily attained by simply dying? A nation that is just and strong is a commonweal of kinsmen, and a volume unimpaired by diseased organs and a morose heart is an equatorial friend. "Call me Ishmael," the opening line of the novel, is prophetic, and I doubt that anybody ever composed as true a one. But we cannot forget that in Scripture the hand of Ishmael, a wild ass of affliction, is against every man's, and every man's against his. Montesquieu wrote, "Men born for society are born to please one another."

Moby-Dick, a verbose, tractarian fable on whaling, is a book of monotonous and unrelenting gloom. Rozanov once said that he did not care for Jesus because He never smiled: in this respect Jesus and Melville have similar dispositions. Melville is more dour than King Saul and there is no harper in the book to assuage his implacable melancholia. Nobody can endure such absolute and unrelieved misery of the spirit and duodenum except the wailing shades by the banks of the Cocytus. What pierces us is not *Moby-Dick*, but the woe in Melville, "the wild, watery loneliness" of his life.

It has been told many times that Herman Melville had an equinoctial identity but that Hawthorne was a wintry prig from Salem. Both were hibernal stylists. Of the two, Melville, perhaps, deceived himself the more and on rare occasions to our advantage, as in the line: "the currents carry ye to those sweet Antilles where the beaches are only beat with water-lilies." However, the soft climes that had made his flesh drowsy had turned his thoughts not to Epicurus but to the anthropophagi. The Tahitian experience had not made him averse to the delights of a cannibal gourmet. Let not the Sirens, who praise Melville for the few lovely lines he composed, take you to the isles already white with the bones of a whole generation of admirers of *Moby-Dick*.

Prometheus stole the fires of Zeus to warm the human race; Melville's sole aim is to thaw those frosts within him. How astonished he was when he remarked: "the blood of a Polar whale is warmer than that of a Borneo negro in summer." Hawthorne had disclosed that human coldness is the worst of all afflictions. Giordano Bruno said that not even the snows of the Alps could cool him, but how seldom are April and May in unverdured, mizzling Melville.

"Can one warm his blue hands by holding them up to the northern lights? Would he not far rather lay him down lengthwise along the line of the equator?" asks Melville. "Would he not be moored to one of the Moluccas?" But this North American Lazarus is lodged, not in Abraham's Bosom, but at the Spouter Inn. His bed companion for the night is not a buxom tavern wench, but a cannibal, Queequeg, "a jolly good bedfellow."

The malady common to both Ishmael and Ahab is unrelieved, warping coldness. Ahab, named after the wicked king who ruled lascivious Samaria, represents the Pilgrim Lotophagi of *terra incognita*. Stendhal, mentioning the Americans, thought that "the source of sensibility is dried up in this people."

Moby-Dick is gigantology, a tract about a gibbous whale, and fifteen or more lawless seamen, who are alone, by choice, though they are together. Ahab is Adam, Cain, Ham, and Nimrod; he is the incarnation of all turpitudes, just as Leviathan is the demiurge and the Pacific the forest of Nôdh; Cain had a beast in his forehead, and Melville writes that Ahab, though evil, has a "crucifixion in his face." In the same wayward vein he claims that the sea is a domestic household at times, and that the sailor experiences a "filial, confident, land-like feeling towards the sea"; Ishmael believes that his bed mate, Queequeg, furnishes him with ease and connubial comfort.

Melville seems to have taken his revenge against the characters in his book as a reprisal for his own solitude. These seafarers have private, mouldy hearts; at the conclusion of this heavy dirge, Ishmael is as alone as he was in the opening pages of *Moby-Dick*. Sir Thomas Browne, whom Melville read avidly, was of the mind that "there is no man alone, because every man is a microcosm."

The characters are scarcely limned at all, except gaunt, miserly Bildad "who . . . sat and never leaned, and this to save his coat tails." When Bildad is considering how small the wages of Ishmael should be, Peleg, fearing he might offer him a few pennies too much, tells him to be wary: "thy conscience may be drawing ten inches of water." Melville abhors both Bildad and Peleg — each is a "magnified species of mouse."

The unmothered, mongrel crew is made up of Nantucketers, sailors from Martha's Vineyard and the Cape, and whalemen from the lands of Asia Minor and of Hamitic Africa. Aside from Starbuck, Stubb, and Flask, the Nantucketers, exsanguious, castaway Cains, who have fished for "crabs and quohogs" on New England's coast, the other main characters, save one Indian from the Vineyard, are Persians, Africans, and Polynesians, those hot men at whose hearth Melville could warm himself.

Stubb, a Capeman, is "neither craven nor valiant." This is the rudest paraphrasis of Revelation: "because thou art lukewarm, and neither cold nor hot, I will spue thee out of my mouth." Starbuck, of Nantucket, is a "long, earnest man"; Flask is "short, ruddy, and young." However, Melville cribs the Polynesian, Indian, Parsee, and the imperial African in his crusty heart. Tashtego, Indian from Gay Head, is the "inheritor of the unvitiated blood of those proud warrior hunters"; Daggoo is a gigantic, Negro Ahasuerus; Fedallah, the Parsee, is a mystic. Melville moans over "black little Pip," "poor Alabama boy." Contradicting himself, he also asserts that "Starbuck, Stubb, and Flask were momentous men." We never find out why. The Carpenter is described as having a "ramifying heartlessness," and is a "stript abstract; an unfractioned integral; uncompromised as a new-born babe." Bulkington, who, as his appellation implies, should have dramatic weight, disappears from the book not long after he enters it, and for no tangible cause. Obviously Melville forgot him altogether. Flagitious

Ahab is dear to Melville; he is evil, but, his author believed, washed in the blood of the lamb. Ahab nods for over half a century of pages. He is wearying because his sorrow is picturesque rather than active; like Milton's Satan, to borrow from Hazlitt, Ahab's deformity is in the depravity of his will.

Herman Melville chose to take the sea, not the fire, or the earth, as his element. "With a philosophical flourish Cato throws himself upon his sword; I quietly take to the ship." Marcus Aurelius said, "Always remember the saying of Heraclitus, that the death of earth is to become water." Heraclitus also reported, "a dry soul is the wisest." Thales said water is the original element and the end. The ancients feared drowning more than any other disaster; there would be no quiet for the deceased in those inscrutable, voracious deeps.

This is a Doomsday book about water. The sea is the foe of Odysseus, the *Odyssey* is the Orphic battle to overcome this moist substance or passion. According to Porphyry, Odysseus desired to "appease his natal daemon with a suppliant branch" of the olive tree of Minerva. Homer, as well as the Greeks, who feared the Ocean, which is the cause of Odysseus' desolation, intends to absolve Odysseus in the end so that he can be with earth-born people "who ne'er knew salt, or heard the billows roar." But Melville is the acolyte of Poseidon and not Minerva. "I am, by a flood, borne back to that wondrous period . . . Here Saturn's grey chaos rolls over me."

The Void made God miserable, and He was unquiet until the waters had receded. The Ocean is too close to Primal Nothing; neither the Cherubim nor men have composure in water, which is the corrupt kindred of nihilism. In the second book of Esdras, Enoch, who is said to be good, is the ruler over dry ground, and Leviathan over the drowned parts of the globe. Adamah, in Hebrew, is virgin red clay, or as Stanley Burnshaw, the poet, says: "All thought is clay / And withered song."

Go to the sea, ye who seek the solace of that immense, empty Bosom, the Ocean, and ye shall lament for the teats, for the pleasant fields, for the fruitful vine. "Do you know that there is not . . . a tree in de Sade?" is an observation in the Goncourts' journals.

Water is a Babel and a confusion in *Moby-Dick*; otherwise, how can we account for Melville's allusions to "sea-pastures," "watery prairies," "Potters' Fields of all four continents," or comprehend "those fabled undulations of the Ephesian sod?" Yet the Deluge is his passion, and he only wrote *justly* when he dealt with the great flood of Noah or Deucalion or the pelagic contents of the universe. The Flood was also for him, as for all early peoples, a punitive disaster.

A plethora of water in the spirit destroys filial affection; Cyclops, who is a son of Neptune and always found on the coast, sins because he cares for nobody, neither the gods nor his parents, save himself, and Euripides considers this his most foul infamy. Whoever sees Cyclops with a wife, children, or a brother? Giants are parricides, and if they have a mother or any kin they are utterly dead to them. The Cyclopian sea-ruffians in the *Pequod* never mention their progenitors. *Moby-Dick* is an unfilial book, and the words thereof are the children in Sheol.

Theophrastus was of the mind that moisture in people was the cause of their stupidity. Tertullian, having no regard for the pagan god of the seas, accepts the ancient claim that the dolphins vomit forth in honor of Neptune. In *Moby-Dick* water is less a natural element than a biblical, allegorical substance. Of the four powers of nature, Melville selected the one that grieved his spirit the most. According to an Egyptian ideograph, water signifies deprivation; the Chinese regarded it as a negative element, and Virgil thought it a deceitful one. Homer said that Oceanus was sterile; Ceres cannot sow wheat here, nor can we find the parsley and the Orphic meadowland surrounding Calypso's cave in *Moby-Dick*. Had Melville been a Hippocrates he would have related that sea water maddens the intellect, makes men splenetic, pituitous, and costive, weakens the large, benevolent organs we have inherited from the Angels who lusted after the fair daughters of men, and gives them instead the hopeless aches of androgynes and eunuchs who are governed by Aquarius. The hermaphrodite rarely laughs, for such boisterous noise is pocketed in that bountiful

123]

Adamic sac, the testes. In Scripture it is written: "Let the waters be gathered to one place, and let dry land appear." But Melville never departed from the seas to return to the earth.

Melville imagined he had taken the paschal lamb of Christ and covered it with the coat of Leviathan. He cringed when he thought of the "universal cannibalism of the ocean, or unverdured seas"— yet most of his volumes are salt-water folios. A hydromaniac, there was very much more of liquid properties than flesh in his prose style. It was in vain that he heaved forth his pain: "Though in many of its aspects this visible world seems formed in love, the invisible spheres were formed in fright."

What is important is not brit, squid, ambergris, or the chapter on Cetology, but Ham's vice, which is the cry of all waters in man. This is the portent of water in *Moby-Dick*. "Yea, foolish mortals, Noah's flood is not yet subsided." God drowned the earth as a judgment of man, for, is it not written in Psalms, "The Lord sat at the Flood"?

The human race perished in the Great Inundation, according to Talmudic Cabalists, because of the intellectual and sexual perversions of mankind. When the Body is false unto itself, the intellect is a liar. *Moby-Dick* is a Hamitic dream; water and meditation are forever married, says the author, and nocturnal visions are damp.

The making of the book took a year; Melville made no corrections, and never rewrote any moiety of it. A novel of over five hundred pages is a great hulking hull. The Canticles of Solomon are short, the book of Ecclesiastes and the Song of Songs a few pages, and how many Hebrew scribes composed and mended these sage and amorous ballads no one will ever know. Who can know all of his errors? Is everything that falls out of the mouth a divine truth? If so, the gabbling women who chase the geese of Camelot are sibyls and canting trimmers are prophets.

In a book of half a millennium of pages, the adjectives alone are heavy enough to sink the Theban Towers, or to borrow from Swinburne: "the eyes which keep open through the perusal of six consecutive pages must never hope to find rest but in the grave." There is more sorrow in his epithets than in the characters, and moreover the adjectives are made to suffer alike on all occasions, for he had a pelting memory and repeated the same desiccated, gothic descriptions frequently.

Only the insane wish to be misologists, and, assuming that one can, at least, read with a tolerable amount of reasonableness, I find no other way of showing how shabbily written *Moby-Dick* is than by adducing the evidence, which is always the "windmills in the brain." What have we of the nature of Ahab but repetitious phrases about his head and mind, which at first may fetch the ear, but later are no more than the specious Elizabethan thunder of a very weary Zeus? The stage roar only deafens us so that all we hear is the monotonous din of surging pages that commenced to roll before the time of Adam, and which do not cease until the readers themselves are drowned in the great Deluge.

At the risk of being a burden of Tyre to the reader I quote the following: Ahab, the ocean, Moby-Dick, and even the *Pequod*, are "moody," "mad," "demonic," "mystic," "brooding," "crazy," "lunatic," "insane," and "malicious." Ahab is stricken, mad, or moody on any page that he is mentioned, and this prolix refrain is likely to send a reader to Bedlam solely to hear a raving inmate declare that he is sane. The brows of Moby-Dick and Ahab are baked in the same kiln of Moloch. Melville had no understanding of heroical size in literature, and tried to achieve the epic by hurling hoaxing, hot phrases at the reader: "Give me Vesuvius' crater for an inkstand!" He attempted to convey the impression that he had large, passionate organs. "Hyperbole is the most frigid of all forms of speech," says Aristotle. Eros is said to have thunderbolts in his right hand, and a trident in his left. Cold must couple with cold, fire with heat, and darkness with night; the fat scum of vice is better than unnatural virtue.

Melville was as luckless with his metaphors, that are nearly always awry and have little connection with the thought in the sentence, as he was with his characters. Had he washed his similes in the Pool of Bethesda they would still be lame and palsied. One might say of Melville what Swinburne said of Byron: "Much of the poem is written throughout in falsetto."

His solecisms and hyperboles are mock fury: "the delta of his forehead's veins," "burnt-out crater of his brain," "Ahab's brow . . . gaunt and ribbed," "globular and ponderous heart," "my splintered heart," "the last gasp of his earthquake life," "he burst his hot heart's shell," "the wondrous cistern in the whale's huge head," "his broad milky forehead," "the whale's huge head," "his pleated head," "his pleated forehead," "his oblong, white head." Ahab and the sperm whale are malevolent monomaniacs: "The white whale . . . as the monomaniac incarnation of all those malicious agencies," "Moby-Dick, with that malicious intelligence," "monomaniac old man," "monomaniac Ahab." Ahab, the Parsee and Leviathan are mystagogues: "the mystic-marked whale" and the Parsee's "mystic watch."

I have told you all there is to know about the characters: Melville discloses in fifty phrases, more or less, that Ahab is a monomaniac. This is scenic diabolism; there is more of Ahab in one line of *Hamlet* than in the entire supernatural allegory: Hamlet speaks, "to define true madness, what is't but to be nothing else but mad"; "I am but mad north-north-west; when the wind is southerly, I know a hawk from a handsaw." Moreover, the tragical writers do not repeatedly say how desolate and broken their heroes are.

This huffing treatise is glutted with: "the whole grim aspect of Ahab," "he was a raving lunatic," "moody, stricken Ahab," "his delirium," "the old man's delirium," "Ahab's full lunacy," "madness sat brooding on his brow," "the whale's direful wrath," "all the subtle demonism of life," "the demoniac waves."

Melville's jadish vocabulary is swollen into the Three Furies, and we flee from them as Ben Jonson in his *Poetaster* took flight from "furibund," "magnificate," "lubrical," "fatuate," "turgidous," "ventosity." For those who are reluctant to believe that such dross is not the customary ailment in this novel, the best advice I can offer is, "Read it yourself, and see."

The atrabilious Ahab is only wicked in the sluttish, supine words with which the author depicts him. Evil is energetic and must accomplish its ends that are just as essential to the Kosmos as the work that good must do.

There is no voyage, and there are no more hints of the characters them-selves than were given at the beginning of the book. We see Ahab either lying in a hammock when the *Pequod* skirts the howling, wet shingle of Patagonia, or standing close to the mizzen shrouds, or upon the quarter-deck leaning on the taffrail. "But in the cautious comprehensiveness and unloitering vigilance . . . Ahab threw his brooding soul into this unfal-tering hunt." Ulysses is a wise, crafty freebooter, but the *Iliad* is a regal poem of action, and the poet justly ascribes "to Ulysses, a thousand gen-erous deeds."

Ahab is no less opaque at the conclusion of the tome than he is at its inception; if, as Shakespeare says in *Lear*, "Ripeness is all," then one can say that in *Moby-Dick*, "Ripeness is nothing." Moreover, we are drinking the waters of Lethe, for Melville did not remember whether he was describ-ing the ocean, the *Pequod*, Ahab, or Leviathan. "The Pequod gored the dark waves in her madness," "great demon of the seas," "all the swift mad-ness of the demoniac waves."

A good deal of bombast has come from the noddles of our intelligentsia about Melville's knowledge of the food and properties of the whale. Con-trary to his usual garrulous habits there are only penurious references to these oceanic viands: "Squid . . . is a vast pulpy mass, furlongs in length . . . twisting like a nest of anacondas," "we fell in with vast meadows of brit, the minute, yellow substance, upon which the Right Whale largely feeds," "ambergris is soft, waxy, and so highly fragrant and spicy, that it is largely used in perfumery, in pastiles, precious candles, hair-powders, and pomatum." Ambergris, according to Melville is "supposed to be the cause . . . of the dyspepsia in the whale."

I should mention a few of the chapter titles and charitably refer to them as a bill of lading of a clerkly Triton sitting in a shipping office on lower Wall Street: "The Chart," "The Try-Works," "The Battering Ram," "The Affidavit," "The Quadrant," "The Monkey-Rope," "Whales in Paint," "The Line," "The Dark," "Pitch-Poling," "Fast Fish and Loose Fish."

There is not the scantiest humdrum minutia omitted: "A belaying pin is found too large to be easily inserted into its hole," "The line . . . used in the fishery was of the best hemp," "while the one tackle is peeling and hoisting a second strip from the whale, the other is slowly slackened away." Malvolio, sometimes called Leon Edel, furnishes us with notes, which are no less baneful than the brackish seawater in *Moby-Dick*: "In Sperm-whalemen with any considerable quantity of oil on board, it is a regular semi-weekly duty to conduct a hose into the hold." In *Moby-Dick* Melville discloses: "But if the doctrine of Fast-Fish be pretty generally applicable, the kindred doctrine of Loose-Fish is still more widely so." Demetrius rebukes those clodpates on Mount Ida who "press home every detail as though your hearer were a fool," and Webster writes: "A fantastical scholar, like such who study to know how many knots was in Hercules' club, or what colour Achilles' beard was." Milton reminds us: "What a stupidness is it, then, that we should deject ourselves to such a sluggish, underfoot philosophy."

Do you want natural history? Then let Aristotle, Pliny, Theophrastus, Dioscorides, Buffon, Darwin, or Humboldt be your masters. Melville's cetology, the science of whales, is borrowed from a hundred books and *Moby-Dick* is only the lees of other men's marine lore. Most of his knowledge came from natural historians, and, like the water wagtail, who pursues the gull until he drops the dung that is the wagtail's principal food, Melville filled himself with the droppings of many volumes on whaling.

We do not study Homer for his nautical information: besides, he knew, perhaps, as little of the sea as Melville did about whaling. One reads Montaigne, Anacreon, Diodorus, Strabo, La Bruyère for pleasure and the intellectual viaticum in wise books. But are chapters on hemp, the pots in which the "hissing masses of blubber" are scalded, and recondite nonsense about old Bible prints of Jonah, a whaling Cabala?

When I want to take a voyage, I don't go to *Moby-Dick*, any more than I read Sir John Mandeville's *Travels* — he wrote about the Holy Land and the ancient world without ever having left England. Mandeville's book is a cento of Pliny, Strabo, Marco Polo, and the refuse of sundry apocryphal Christian works. If you would travel, then go to the journals of voyages compiled by Hakluyt, or wander through the marvelous pages collected by Purchas, or take up rough Drake, or Pigafetta's Magellan as your guide.

However, so many of the borrowed facts about the habits of whales are of no unusual significance, anyway, in a novel or a work of the imagination. I am unable to enumerate the piscatory errors in Izaak Walton's *The Compleat Angler*, but I read him for his style, which is another name for perception or wisdom. The thoughts we have are only the words we use. Melville's sentences, however, are always to the windward, so that the reader is worn out by the heavy, ululant blasts of his fraudulent blank verse. Form is the real food of the imagination; facts are the stepdaughters of the muses.

Melville writes: "The previous chapter gave account of an immense body or herd of Sperm Whales," which is gawkish advice to his auditors who, he imagines, could not even recollect a single chapter fifteen minutes after reading it. But how often we reprove others for our own faults. Hesiod thought that Zeus lay with Mnemosyne, who is Memory and the mother of muses, for nine days and nine nights without interruption; and it requires that much Olympian, not whale, sperm to fecundate the intellect. Melville had never gone to Delphi to comprehend the best of admonitions: "Know thyself." A novelist, he had almost no knowledge of people. What we call knowledge of others is what we know about ourselves.

How much more fortunate is his short, but renowned chapter, "The Whiteness of the Whale"? There is the same melancholia in it as in the rest of the novel. Though Moby-Dick is priapic Jupiter, the snow-white bull, white represents death. The Albatross in those "exiled waters" is a portentous wraith, and "the White Mountains of New Hampshire," are "a gigantic ghostliness" that hangs over his gray, hulled soul. "The White Sea exerts such a spectralness over the fancy." "Witness the white bear of the poles, and the white shark of the tropics . . . transcendent horrors they are." St. John the Evangelist rides on his pallid horse and the fierce-fanged tiger wears the same mortuary vesture, and Lima, a lepry city of sin "has taken the white veil"; "all deified Nature absolutely paints like the harlot, whose allurements cover nothing but the charnel-house within." Melville concludes this white Golgotha with: "And of all these things the Albino whale was the symbol. Wonder ye then at the fiery hunt?" Of course, he is again paraphrasing Revelation: "And I looked, and behold a pale horse: and his name that sat on him was Death."

Compare this with Rabelais, who, grounded in ancient lore, reminds us that the Thracians and Greeks marked their "good, propitious and fortunate days with white stones." Gargantua wears Jovean, white slops trimmed with blue, which contain eleven hundred and five ells of phallus, bacon, tripes, roasted thrushes basted with hen-scum and wine. Paris was formerly called, Rabelais avers, Leucotia, in honor of the white thighs of the women there.

When the Archangel Raphael appears before Tobit, the latter announces that there is nothing so good and comforting as Light, which is the raiment of the Cherubim. Allen Tate writes that for Dante "Light is Beatrice; light is her *smile*." Alba, the sacred first town in Latium, was founded by Aeneas where the white sow sat down to rest. Such a legend signifies gestation, the keeping-room and the house, but who breeds porkers or reaps wheat in the Pacific?

However, it is now time for more citations.

this strange uncompromisedness in him involved a sort of unintelligence.

To insure the greatest efficiency in the dart, the harpooneers of this world must start to their feet out of idleness.

[The carpenter] was singularly efficient in those thousand nameless mechanical emergencies continually recurring in a large ship.

this omni-tooled, open-and-shut carpenter.

these spiritual throes in him heaved his being up from its base, and a chasm seemed opening in him, from which forked flames and lightnings shot up.

crazy Ahab, the scheming, unappeasedly steadfast hunger of the white whale; this Ahab . . . had gone to his hammock.

Here be it said, that this pertinacious pursuit of one particular whale, continued through day into night, and through night into day.

little Flask bobbed up and down like an empty vial.

He was like one of those unreasoning but still highly useful, *multum in parvo*, Sheffield contrivances.

this half-horrible stolidity in him, involving, too, as it appeared, an all-ramifying heartlessness; — yet was it oddly dashed at times, with an old, crutch-like, antediluvian, wheezing humorousness, not unstreaked now and then with a certain grizzled wittiness.

however promissory of life and passion in the end, it is above all things requisite that temporary interests and employments should intervene and hold them healthily suspended for the final dash.

There are some enterprises in which a careful disorderliness is the true method.

Is this the "honest manna of literature"?

But may nobody believe that I would conceal the chants of a man who had enough genius to sing on occasion, but not sufficient strength to write an epical novel. A good sentence or emotion in *Moby-Dick* will come as dear as the cost of dove's dung at the time of the famine in Samaria. Here are some of Melville's canorous lines:

I leave a white and turbid wake; pale waters, paler cheeks, where'er I sail. The envious billows sidelong swell to whelm my track; let them; but first I pass.

Yonder, by the ever-brimming goblet's rim, the warm waves blush like wine. The gold bow plumbs the blue.

But it is a mild, mild wind, and a mild looking sky; and the air smells now, as if it blew from a far-away meadow; they have been making hay somewhere under the slopes of the Andes, Starbuck, and the mowers are sleeping among the new-mown hay. Sleeping? Aye, toil we how we may, we all sleep at last on the field. Sleep? Aye, and rust amid greenness; as last year's scythes flung down, and left in the half-cut swaths . . .

let me look into a human eye; it is better than to gaze into sea or sky; better than to gaze upon God. By the green land; by the bright hearth-stone! this is the magic glass . . .

There is a wisdom that is woe; but there is a woe that is madness. And there is a Catskill eagle in some souls . . .

Oh, grassy glades! oh, ever vernal endless landscapes in the soul; in ye, — though long parched by the dead drought of the earthly life, — in ye, men yet may roll, like young horses in new morning clover. . . . Would to God these blessed calms would last.

American literature is exceedingly poor in victuals and in amours. No character has been adequately fed or loved in an American novel for a hundred and twenty-five years. The sailors on the *Pequod* seem as content with biscuit and ship's beef as Cyclops, a part-time vegetarian monster, is with curds and cow's milk. But the Colossus of Euripides prefers a roasted stag, a lion on the spit, or gobbets of human flesh. A heathen's collation on the *Pequod* consists of large gammons of whale blubber. These mariners have the gloomy, Phrygian throats of Bacchanal nymphs who milked a lioness and made cheese of the milk. Melville knew no subtler delicacy of the table than strawberries swimming in the milk of the sperm whale. The author thought that "brains of a small Sperm Whale are accounted a fine dish." "The casket of the skull is broken into with an axe, and the two plump, whitish lobes being withdrawn (precisely resembling two large puddings), they are then mixed with flour, and cooked into a most delectable mess." "The imagination is wounded long before the conscience" is a wise thought from Henry David Thoreau.

What wry joy does this descendant of Ham and Polyphemus, perverse in all of his appetites, take in telling the reader of those profane, Polynesian meals of human flesh: the barbecued heads that had been decapitated by cannibals in Tahiti "were placed in great wooden trenchers, and garnished round like a pilau, with breadfruit and cocoanuts; and with some parsley in their mouths." Aristotle advises the poet that not everything can be divulged, or offered in plain view "lest Medea murder her children in front of the audience, or impious Atreus cook human flesh in public."

Whose gorge is not qualmish as he witnesses Stubb eating his "spermaceti supper" as "thousands on thousands of sharks" are swarming round the dead whale roped to the *Pequod*? What froward humor there is in Melville when he places before the reader "a meat pie nearly one hundred feet long" made of the innards of a whale. So much blubber gives one indigestion for "the rest of his reading days."

There is no doxy, trollop, or trull in any of Melville's volumes. He had no likerish palate; even chaste Spenser would allow the desolate tribe of males the solace of "her snowy breast was bare to greedy spoil." Moreover, who, after such an incubus, does not pine to hear the sound of her petticoats, the sweet, nourishing sight of her licentious skirts? After considering the intricate intestines of a sperm whale, as Melville advises us to do, I am as ready as Holofernes to swoon when I behold Judith's sandals.

Samuel Daniel pined for Delia, Swift wrote memorable epistles to Stella, and the singers in Israel were pierced by those maids who had eyes like the fishpools of Heshbon, but Melville lays bare the beams, the joists, the sinews of a whale. Montesquieu told his friends that the only reason he wrote was to seek favor with the Venuses at court. Herman Melville at the age of thirty, when he should have been an amorist, was as gloomy as John Donne who sat in his shroud after he had passed his fiftieth year.

None can misdoubt Melville's misogyny. The hatred of women is the pederastic nausea that comes from the mention of the womb. Robert Burton, in *The Anatomy of Melancholy*, says that a Muscovite Duke vomited when he saw a woman. Melville, Whitman, Poe, and Thoreau loathed the female, and the first three sages suffered from sodomy of the heart. No more than three generations separate us from Thoreau, Whitman, Poe, and Melville; little wonder then that we are now in the age of ice, and that one man in every ten craves to burn in the fires of Sodom and Gomorrah.

Instead of all those spermal ablutions for the pathic, in which Melville said the male should wash his heart, give me the Restoration wit of: "Two years' marriage has debauched my five senses. Everything I see, everything I hear, everything I feel, everything I smell, and everything I taste, methinks has wife in it." "Methinks my body is but the lees of my better being," declares Melville. At Sais the peplum of Isis was never lifted, and in sixteen volumes by Melville no woman is bedded, seduced, or gulled, and, by heaven, that is gross deception.

Perversity is the black angel of our century, and the hatred of the clan of females, so deep in Melville, Poe, Whitman, and Thoreau, is our Atlean inheritance which we must understand or perish. Eros is the source of masculine life and wit; what there is of gaiety in American letters is either

133]

puerile or those few parched, sly conceits in *Moby-Dick* and *Bartleby the Scrivener.*

Melville's "If ye touch at the islands, Mr. Flask, beware of fornication," is a wry imitation of Paul's admonition to the Colossians: "avoid fornication, impurity, lust, evil concupiscence." Melville's line is likely to produce a pewed smile, but far better and more jovial is Rabelais' Bumpkin who keeps the Psalter in his codpiece.

Who wants to chase a Sperm-Whale for over five hundred pages when he can pursue a Shulamite, a Cressid, a dowdy, or a shake-bag? Had Herman Melville never been moved by amorous ballads? Can a dolphin, a chine of blubber, or the white hump of a whale take the place of the thighs of Aspasia or the rump of Lais of Corinth? This is Melville's phallic song: "Other poets have warbled . . . the soft eyes of the antelope . . . less celestial, I celebrate a tail [of Leviathan]."

Melville composed amorous canticles to an oceanic brute, and the sea was his hymeneal bed. Leviathan is a "luxurious Ottoman," with "all the solaces and endearments of the harem"; the Sperm Whale has a "beautiful and chaste-looking mouth . . . glossy as bridal satins." The pelagic brutes are "unprincipled young rakes"; Leviathan is a "Lothario, like pious Solomon among his thousand concubines."

What else are "the submarine bridal chambers of Leviathan," and all those spermal remedies that he said Paracelsus advised the ill to take to allay their wrath, than epithalamiums? Though Melville could not reject the old Hebrew law of retribution, he had little of that masculine fire in him; Empedokles believed that "in its warmer part the womb brings forth males."

Ahab's solipsism comes from the pride of Narcissus, and there is no hemlock so pernicious as the arts of self-love. Ahab represents moisture, and in the Psalms it is "the proud water." "Blind is the man who does not hate self-love," said the author of the *Pensées.* What reason has Narcissus to regard a woman when he finds so much satisfaction in contemplating his own face?

Woman is still the imperial booty of the races, and men will sack towns,

[134

capture cities to furnish their courtesans with money to purchase cosmetics and soap, or rape the Sabine virgins when they cannot obtain wives otherwise. Plato knew that nothing was so acute as the pleasures of the body, without which men will hanker for a whale, a dog, a cat, and go stark mad to be like "that lecher that carneled with a statue." Origen horrified the Christian Fathers by castrating himself although they were intellectual wethers themselves. Men suffer either because they have testes or because they have none.

Rather than dissect the corpse of one woman, which Balzac advises the novice in amours to do, before he selects a wife, Melville offers the American the anatomy of Leviathan. Here is the cause of Melville's woe, and ours. He wrote a book for men, or, at least, hermaphrodites and spados. I would just as lief reread *Moby-Dick* as live in a volume or a world without any females in it.

Woman is a perfidious creature in *Moby-Dick*, and he cannot refer to Judith or Cleopatra without giving the impression that it was not Holofernes nor Antony who was betrayed but Herman Melville. In an allusion that has no reasonable connection with the sentence or the chapter he speaks of the gory head of Holofernes hanging from the girdle of Judith. "Towards noon whales were raised . . . they turned and fled . . . a disordered flight, as of Cleopatra's barges from Actium." When Melville writes of Jupiter abducting Europa, his sole interest is in the "lovely, leering eyes" of Zeus; of Europa he says nothing. "By Jupiter, I must not fear a woman," say Beaumont and Fletcher in *The Philaster*.

Melville believed Sir Thomas Browne who wrote that woman is "the rib and the crooked piece of Man," and that "man is the whole world, and the breath of God," which, if true, indicates that there is something amiss in the Lord's respiration. The mariners of the *Pequod*, like Adam, must have been "born without a navel," for none appears to have a mother; all are either unwived or unsocial, despite the few reluctant references to those "far-away domestic memories" that afflict Ahab, a "houseless, family-less, old man."

After the blubber pots and the love scenes of these corrugated, mammoth Don Juans of the sea, what virile male reader does not yearn for the witty bouts between a smell-smock and a flirt, or a sweet bosom that would set Ilium on fire? Whatever Sir John Brute is aching for it is not the Ephesian dugs of a whale, the matrix of a porpoise, or the oceanic marriage bed of Leviathan. Wycherley's Dorilant has enough wit to penetrate the most amiable feminine heart: "A mistress should be like a little country retreat near the town; not to dwell in constantly, but only for a night, and away, to taste the town the better when a man returns."

The Roman virgin sat on the image of the phallus; in Egypt at the time of Philadelphus Ptolomey there was a festival in which the matrons carried Priapus who was a hundred and twenty-five cubits in length, and that is as long as a seminal book should be. Now that we are prepared to hawk this divine god, Priapus, let us announce that what we are willing to sell, barter, or even give away is, *For Women Only*.

What nature makes us we are; contend with this absolute force at the risk of your sanity. A virile male craves his opposite, and that is nature and habit which are the parents of morals. The wise Rabbin said that the contemporaries of Noah were defiant sinners, and drove the Shekinah away from the world.

At the risk of sowing dragon's teeth, and acquiring another legion of foes I have never seen, I must impugn *Moby-Dick* as inhuman literature. What kind of a moral novel is this? Alas, the word moral has been the shibboleth of the philister. That gentle genius, Herbert Read, mislikes this word, and prefers justice in the place of it, but what will prevent the academic presbyters of literature from pre-empting this word, too?

Who worships vice, arrogance, or a brute of the salty deep? Since the beasts and demons are within man, what need is there to pursue them? Nobody should resolve to be vile: "See! Moby-Dick seeks thee not. It is thou, thou that madly seekest him!" What is bad will fall out of the soul anyway. Who looks everywhere for trouble? In Proverbs it is stated: "A prudent man seeth evil, and hideth himself." Jesus goes into the wilderness to withstand temptation, but the Gospels are gray, plain truths. Moreover, who wants to be worse than he already is? And who would not care to obey Ben Jonson's maxim, "He that for love of goodness hateth ill."

Goodness did not tempt Melville sorely. Pascal says that "Milton is well aware that Nature is corrupt and that men are hostile to morality." Melville, a Pauline invert, remarks: "Bethink thee of that saying of St. Paul in Corinthians, about corruption and incorruption; how that we are sown in dishonor, but raised in glory."

We only recognize men's virtues when they benefit us. Moreover, morals which do not come from a concupiscent nature are a cold wind upon the frail, reedy spirit. He who is in agony because he is not hot hankers for the fabled Apples of Sodom.

Melville was unable to understand St. Paul because he himself was the prey of corrosive acedy. The work of the moth and rust had deprived him of energy, without which morality is a basilisk. "For the flesh lusteth against the Spirit, and the Spirit against the flesh." No one can avoid this battle, whether he be a hedonist or have strong ascetic inclinations, lest he be a viper to his brother and detest everybody for no other reason than his reluctance to overcome his faults. One who has tepid or cold privities can never pardon anybody, especially those whom he has harmed. Worse, he regards the human race as his foe, though in his secret soul he knows the real adversary is himself.

It is told that Paul fought with the beasts at Ephesus; but with what sort of clandestine lust was Herman Melville concerned in *Moby-Dick*? What turpitude does he wish to drown in the great Deluge?

Says Seneca: "A man may dispute, cite great authorities, talk learnedly, huff it out, and yet be rotten at heart."

We are not dealing with Melville's torn, empirical life, but with his imagination, which is the truest experience. Men reveal themselves most when they dream, and Moby-Dick is the Titanic sodomite serpent that crept into his dark, blighted heart, never to quit that lair in which the most abominable passions lurk, as we see in his last, homosexual, work, *Billy Budd*.

Though he has been somewhat touched by that dreariest of screeds, the perfectibility of man —"immaculate manliness" is what Melville calls it — one can look in vain for a piacular sentence in *Moby-Dick*. But what savant does not talk as though his heart were not decayed? St. Paul and Pascal spoke simply, never failing to understand that they suffered because they were obsessed by foul imaginings, a truth that Herman Melville never understood. So much of our lives is given over to the consideration of our imperfections that there is no time to improve our imaginary virtues. The truth is we only perfect our vices, and man is a worse creature when he dies than he was when he was born: "and Jesus said, Why callest thou me good? None is good." Men cocker their vices and whatever they do that is good is the consequence of vanity, and thoughtlessness: he is born stupid and dies depraved. Christ sent his lambs to go among the wolves, and Moby-Dick is no lamb.

Ahab does not seek glory but scrapes the bottom of Tartarus and all obscure depths for infamy. The Puritan is a clandestine lecher, and dreams are beasts that come in the night; *Moby-Dick* is the vision of the noctambulist and a furtive, dark trance. Ishmael, Ahab, Daggoo, Queequeg, Pip, Fedallah, Tashtego, the detritus of Tartary and Asia Minor, are symbols of nocturnal orgies. Moby-Dick is a primordial animal, and his watery home is the Pacific, which is an Asiatic ocean, for the first peoples came to the new world over this vasty stream. Leviathan is one of the Minotaurs, Sphinxes, and Centaurs, which Plutarch thought were the products of the monstrous, incestuous, and ungovernable lusts of man.

Melville abhorred nature, and thought that God was not the peer of the demiurge, who, as one of the ante-Nicene Fathers held, was the cause of corruption and death. The Gnostics also referred to Sophia as the Spirit and the Demiurge as the Devil. The suffering atheists, or self-gnawing agnostics, who composed the Book of Job, had the same conception.

The author of the Zohar said that before Noah there were only three just men in the earth, Methuselah, Enoch, and Jared, and who can forget that Noah is the father of the first sodomite, Ham? Moreover, who has not the most acute compassion for Herman Melville's ontological pain? Had not the prophet Jeremiah also cried out in anguish: "O Lord, Thou hast deceived us," and does not Jesus in a rueful, gnostical mood lament: "Your Father is a murderer from the beginning"? What concerns us is that Melville was a perverted Christian, and that the tawdry writing in *Moby-Dick* is to some extent willful self-hatred.

Herman Melville had committed sodomy, as it is meant in the Old Testament; in his mind he had had connection with a beast of the deep. Take woman from man and he will yearn for an angel, a porpoise, a whale. This starveling became a hunter for profane and nether flesh, dolphins, sharks, leviathan, and man, whatever could ease those clinkered, lava lusts. Unable to be consumed in the flames of Troy for Helen, he was cindered in the fires of Sodom and Gomorrah. Read his last work, *Billy Budd*, a piece of inverted mariolatry, for it is the virgin boy, Budd, the name of a maiden, who is his Mary.

The only real marriage in the book is between Queequeg and Ishmael. "He pressed his forehead against mine, clasped me round the waist, and said that henceforth we were married." "No place like a bed for confidential disclosures," and this is as close to the bed of Venus as he ever comes.

Melville's Christ is "soft, curled, hermaphroditical," "negative" and "feminine." Give us a pagan Christ, in part Apis and Mnevis! Why does Jesus wear a loincloth? The women at Pompeii substituted the cross for the image of the phallus they had worn around their necks. The crucifix hangs against the fertile paps of the Catholic virgin, and what natural woman carries the image of a man close to her carnal bosom without sensual pangs? We must cast out such diabolical conceptions of goodness, as the Lord himself "opens the kingdoms of heaven to eunuchs," and "it remains, that they who have wives so be as if they have not" or there will be a universal Sodom and Gomorrah.

Melville is an Ophite and his supernatural whale, "the starry Cetus," is a species of Dagon, the fish-like deity of the Philistines. The whale, though a mammal, was a great fish and a serpent to the ancient fabulists, and Christ is a moist star — Jesus is Pisces.

Leviathan in the Zohar is feminine. The Leviathan, the oldest foe of

139]

man, is called Rahab by Isaiah and the Psalmist — the Dragon and the serpent. "Thou hast broken Rahab in pieces" and "Art thou it that hath cut Rahab and wounded the dragon?" both come from Isaiah and refer to a feminine creature, and is not Rahab also the whore of Jericho? Elohim, too, is often feminine in the Cabala and in Gnostic theology. Proclus in the *Timaeus* believed that "Nature is suspended from the back of the vivifying goddess." The female part of God was known as the Shekinah to the cabalistical thinkers. Clement of Alexandria writes that the symbol of the Bacchic orgies is a consecrated reptile and also that the name Hevia, or Eve, signifies a female serpent.

But for Melville, a superstitious scientist, or a Talmudic one, the pelagic Demiurge is masculine. His mammoth, in part, is one of the "monsters of Rahab" of the olden Rabbin; Leviathan is Tiamat of the Gilgamesh epic, the dragon of Isaiah, the Psalmist, Job, and Enoch. *Moby-Dick* is a hybrid of Scripture and zoology, and this brute of the sea is the product of the "half-foetal suggestions of supernatural agencies." Thomas Traherne wrote that "to call things preternatural Natural is Monstrous."

Osiris, the personification of the generative organs of man to the Egyptians, was second in importance to Isis, the begetter. She is the Ancient One just as God is known as the Ancient of Days in the Book of Daniel. It is Isis, the goddess, and not the aboriginal hermaphrodite, masculine in front, but feminine in the hinder parts, who is searching all the waters of the Nile for the genitals of her consort. Did she find them, or are we men with only a tithe of a prepuce?

However, it is the spermal deity Melville worships, not the Generatrix, as is apparent in one of Melville's extraordinary raptures: "In thoughts of the visions of the night, I saw long rows of angels in paradise, each with his hands in a jar of spermaceti." Of the sperm Melville writes: "I washed my hands and my heart [in] it."

In spite of the fact that the novel is a doxology of a wicked beast of the seas, Melville believed in punishment, for the *Pequod* is a "whited sepulchre" on the outside, but full of "dead men's bones within." Furthermore, in the Cabala it is explained that the human race perished, save Noah and his family, by drowning. But why was homosexual Ham spared, and does not Melville follow the same parable since all die by water save Ishmael, who is really Ham? And the universal Hamite is grum, aqueous, and froward.

Moby-Dick is Christian zoolatry, a Puritanical bestiary, and in some respects, not dissimilar from the Egyptian *Book of the Dead*. Philo Judeaus had rebuked the Egyptians for their idolatry of crocodiles, dogs, the ibis, and cats. In ancient Cairo superannuated cats were fed in charity hospitals. One cat in a house is a sign of loneliness, two of barrenness, and three of sodomy. *Moby-Dick* is the bestial Bible of modern Ham.

The dark races awakened his concupiscence: is not Ham the Father of Africa? Melville called his seafarers mermen. Only dark or olive flesh stirred in him the ashes of Borsippa, Ur, and Canaan. Ham is also the father of Canaan who is the primal forebear of the Canaanites who were destroyed because of their terrible wantonness. The "imperial" Negro Daggoo was his phallic idol, and the name was obviously derived from Dagon, a god with the tail of a fish. There were Tashtego, black Pip whom he fondles, and Fedallah the Parsee who is the only one before whom Ahab stands in awe. Water is vice, retribution, and Ham; the spermal whale is Priapus who has deprived Ahab of his phallical leg. As Fedallah is drowning, Ahab, for no overt cause, moans for the "unforgiven ghosts of Gomorrah." The words in the soul rise to the lips on a sudden, because no lust can sink them. Ay, it is a dry, dry book in which a man can drown all his sins.

These are seafaring Nimrods; Nimrod is the hunter whose iniquity is his pride, and the *Pequod* is a Babel, as Melville shows in the chapter "Midnight, Forecastle"; it is the Tower of Hubris on the watery plains of Shinar.

Since we are as bad as our dreams, and our books are no better, it was inevitable that Melville should have had Cyclops' anthropophagous palate, and that after *Moby-Dick* he should have written *Pierre*, a novel about incest. Those meager sentences that are supposed to be cetology in *Moby-Dick* are very close to quack erudition because there is a failure in sensibility and a drought of the organs of the body. We can only write well about our sins because it is too difficult to recall a virtuous act or even whether it was the result of good or evil motives.

There is now a pederastic hagiography composed of people who prefer the bad to the good, who like excrements instead of pond-apples, sumach, dogwood, or hyacinths, and who choose men rather than women to be their paramours. Intellectual sodomy, which comes from the refusal to be simple about plain matters, is as gross and abundant today as sexual perversion and they are nowise different from one another. This kind of pathic in literature has wan, epicene affections. A misologist, he takes ophidian pleasure in the misuse of words, and his sacerdotal gibberish sounds more like the cries of animals than the holy Logos or the alphabet of the god Thoth. Is there a genius in Christendom whose holy credo is not: "In the beginning was the Word"? Specious rebels, they are the advocates of the rabble arts.

The martyrology of the sodomite consists of St. Ordure, St. Incest, and St. Matricide. The inverted Christian eremite nowadays has a matricidal heart, and is either totally separated from his parents, or utterly detests them. How feeble is the image of the father in nineteenth-century American literature; had Poe any parents at all? What do we know of Melville's male progenitor, or Whitman's, and was the great savant, Thoreau, born of stocks and stones? The misogamist spawns the homosexual, and *Moby-Dick* is the worship of the male sperm. Phallic idolatry is the concern of women, and no literature can be bawdy, human, and sage unless men love women; no nation can survive, not Hellas nor Jerusalem, when the stews for males are substituted for the hetaira and the olive-complexioned damsels who were the solace of the harper and his son, the amorist Solomon.

ALLEN TATE, THE FORLORN DEMON

"IS LITERARY CRITICISM POSSIBLE?" Allen Tate queries.
There is a noble despair in this question and those who refuse to ask it are
pragmatic "porkers in tears." That we do not know what we think we know
is no quibble; it is the tragedy of man endeavoring to attain knowledge that
is beyond the powers of his feeble intellect. Let me then, as I commence
this essay upon Allen Tate, admit that I am a Sisyphean failure, for whatever words I may roll up the Cordilleras will fall down on my head again.

Tate has elected to examine the *Biographia Literaria*. At the beginning
one should first pay tribute to Samuel Taylor Coleridge and freely own that
we have garnered much from him; William Hazlitt has written that Coleridge was the only person from whom he ever learned anything.

Tate quotes a passage from the *Biographia Literaria* that is rather typical of that volume: "A poem is that species of composition, which is opposed to works of science, by proposing for its *immediate* object pleasure,
not truth; and from all other species — (having this object in common with
it) — it is distinguished by proposing to itself such delight from the whole,

143]

as is compatible with a distinct gratification from each component part." Aside from the dull, hydropic iterations, and the false gigantic weight of the word species, what is there in this that does not enervate the mind, and take advantage of the trusting eyes?

The above is ambiguous grammar and a cumbersome syntax pampered into a kind of doctrine of truth and beauty. Whether a poem is a moral exhortation or should be written to give pleasure is a squab commonplace. One cannot avoid being a sophister as well as a noddy by attempting to find out what is in the poet's mind as he labors for his precise numbers.

Once the critic assumes that it is possible to define pleasure or truth, or what Tate would call the "machine of sensations," he is erecting an epistemological Babel. Since knowledge is chimerical, the academic stench is more horrid when the cabala of grammar is passed off as metaphysics. This pinchbeck diction comes, as Tate views it, from the "critic's own intellectual pride." The good and just use of words fires our entrails and hopes, while wandering phrases which cannot explain themselves make cowards of us. How many have lain in the dust after perusing the jargon of aesthetics? The critic, having a niggish skill with words, and pretending that the buskined gait of the tragedian is contemptible, adopts the mock elevated style of the philosopher and scientist. As Tate remarks: "the philosophical language in which he . . . expounds the insight may seem to reflect an authority that he has not visibly earned."

The result is that a scholion written upon Homer is harder to understand than the *Iliad*. Tate writes: "The . . . form of the . . . poem, the novel . . . lies neglected on the hither side of the Styx, where Virgil explains to Dante that it is scorned alike by heaven and hell." That one cannot go from the elaborate exegesis to the Greek epic is obvious. What is then culled from Aristotle, Longinus, Porphyry, Dryden, and Coleridge seldom illuminates the plays of Euripides, or of Ben Jonson, or John Webster. Of course, nobody has ever been able to explain a poem; after the critic has cut an elegy or an ode into collops, the most he can offer is a random perception or show us a few lines we have missed. Dryden held that "To read Macrobius, explaining the propriety and elegancy of many words in Virgil, which I had before passed over without consideration as common things, is enough to assure me that I ought to think the same of Terence." Otherwise, the literary critic is as impotent in conveying the whole of the *Iliad* as Ulysses was in grasping the ghost of Anticlea.

At least half of the *Biographia Literaria* is morose Kantian verbiage. It cannot be said that Coleridge's Germanized English is any more baleful than Kant's olympian trash on aesthetics. To peruse the treatise by Immanuel Kant on that subject is an atlean misfortune; before the reader has loaded his duodenum with twenty-five pages of it he is brought to bed and wondering why the study of beauty should be uttered in such besotted polysyllables. One has no better luck with Schiller, Goethe, Bosanquet, Croce, or I. A. Richards.

In spite of his abilities, Coleridge had a lazy, fat-witted ear; he lacked a goatish appetite for English. Had Coleridge overlooked, or was he too sublime to comprehend, what Thomas Campion had to say about English *poesie* — that it stands "chiefly on monosillables"? The same can be alleged of prose. Herbert Read, though deeply affected by the *Biographia Literaria*, is the author of *Annals of Innocence*, a well-nigh faultless pastoral poem which seldom exceeds a dissyllable.

The auricular and sensual pleasure received from a poem is usually far more acute than that from prose. But the hearer should be rapt in love with either. There is a heap of pedagogical dross in the marvelous dramatic essays of Dryden, but also enough of the simple, parboiled idiom to take care of a humble reader's commons. One is sure to have good fortune with Swift. The *Journal to Stella* could have been penned by a servantmaid were she a prose stylist. The ideas in this epistolary diary concern a rasher of bacon on the coals, what hour the hackney coach arrived, who had the quartain ague or gout, and whether the Dean had a Nestorian bumper of wine for his supper. However, Jonathan Swift's colloquial language will satisfy the heroic gut of any prentice in prosody or well-shaped conceits.

To return to the author of the *Biographia Literaria*: In the most brilliant description of Coleridge I have ever read, Tate alludes to him as "a Teutonic angel inhabiting a Cartesian machine." Again Tate quotes Coleridge:

"The first chapter of Isaiah — (indeed a very large portion of the whole book) — is poetry in the most emphatic sense; yet it would be no less irrational than strange to assert, that pleasure, not truth, was the immediate object of the prophet." For the moment, without troubling about this huffing platitude, and the cumbersome parenthesis within the period, compare it with a brace of homely lines, one from Spenser and the other from Traherne. Though both can be reckoned as no less obvious, who would gainsay that they are not far more savory: "So now fayre Rosalind hath bredde hys smart" and "They put Grubs and Worms in Mens Heads."

Suppose now we scrutinize this sentence of the "simple-minded Evangelist," as Tate refers to him. Few would trouble to deny that the sundry Hebrew scribes who composed the chapters of Isaiah were poets though they were unfamiliar with the iambics of Archilochus or the blank verse of Surrey. After pondering these quibbles is it amiss to ask what Coleridge meant by pleasure — that barnacle that cleaves to truth and hope? For example, was Sir Walter Raleigh's "Give me my scallop shell of quiet" writ to balm his own flagging spirit, or to furnish others with faith or joy? What at first blush appears to be an exhortation is an exquisite dolor. Resolution in any poet is only the draff of a fleeting moral conception. Who can know human flesh? Human nature is as enigmatic as the salt sea that beats itself against the shingle, or as protean as the moods of gneiss or the intellectual operations of the Pyrenees.

Tate himself is on occasion as abstruse as the naiads who weave orphic arguments on their stony looms. In his reveries, speaking almost to himself, he says that he is not sure that we need a "philosophical aesthetics in order to produce a work of art." Milton epistled his *Samson Agonistes* with some grave remarks about Aristotle, but what connection is there between *Samson Agonistes* and the *Poetics*? We may also ask what is the relation between Porphyry's chapbook and the *Odyssey*? After going over Porphyry's orphic view of the cave at Phorcys we may give far more attention to grottos and the naiads inside them, but can one believe that Porphyry's esoteric remarks about the cavern where Ulysses went when he came ashore had anything to do with the *Odyssey*? No matter how much of Aristotle, Longinus, or Porphyry the poet imbibes, as soon as he commences to make the poem, he is whelmed in Lethe's flood. Gorged with erudite oblivion he is prepared for the dionysiac frenzy. The more we forget the closer are we to nature's malefic purpose, our demise; and uttering a poem is a "Steadie aiming at a tomb" — George Herbert.

The whole quandary of literary criticism lies on the head of Allen Tate like the Andes; he claims that the commentaries may become "dogmatic when the critic achieves a coherence in the logical and rhetorical orders which exceed the coherence of the imaginative work itself."

In Tate's parlous chapter "Longinus and the 'New Criticism,'" he observes that the "Height of Eloquence" is a more exact title for Longinus's book than "On the Sublime." He also adds that the two principal themes in Longinus's peroration are elevation of language and transport. Although not unmindful of the pedantry, Tate acknowledges that he "cannot expect to disentangle them from each other." In a similar pedagogic vein Tate writes: "To allegorize infinite magnitude, quantity beyond the range of the eyes, is to reduce it to the scale of what Kant called the Beautiful as distinguished from the Sublime." Now either this is logomachy, or my inability to paraphrase, or a weakness of intellect on my part.

Whatever the above may mean, Kant and Tate have spun a finer web than Arachne could. As for me, I will never know the difference between the sublime and the beautiful. I'd rather view it as Eric Gill did when he said: "I think I have said it often . . . that a pendant on the neck is useful and possibly more so than a trouser button." For me Wordsworth's poetry is the trouser button and Sir Walter Raleigh's verse is a pendant, and that is the best I can do. If I risk more than such an unambitious metaphor, I am in epistemological trouble. Or to put the whole matter quite bluntly, I don't know what I am talking about.

The cause of so much newfangled ignorant verbosity is, as Tate observes, the result of hubris; the misuse of words comes from the doctrine of pride. Aside from the vain pomp of language that goes with a specious misology there is what Tate refers to as the "three classical faculties, feeling, will, and intellect." This triune is as much of a fable as the father, the son, and the holy ghost. Tate expresses it thus: "There is little doubt that Coleridge's failure to get out of the dilemma of Intellect-or-Feeling has been passed on to us as a fatal legacy." Tate has occasion to allude to the following muddled sentence of Henry James: "The writer who cultivates his instinct rather than his awareness sits by finally in a stale and shrinking puddle." Is it idle to wonder how anyone can plow and seed his instinct while allowing his awareness to lie fallow?

We are involved in the same absurd syntax in Eliot's description of Edgar Poe cited by Allen Tate. Eliot says that Poe "appears to yield himself completely to the idea of the moment: the effect is, that all his ideas seem to be entertained rather than believed. What is lacking is not brainpower, but that maturity of intellect which comes only with the maturing of a man as a whole, the development and coordination of the various emotions." "I am surprised," comments Tate, "that Mr. Eliot seems to assume that *coordination* of the 'various emotions' is ever possible." Eliot is exhaling false prophetic vapors: what does he mean by "maturity of intellect . . . comes only with the maturity of man as a whole"? This suggests that man sometimes only thinks with a parcel of his skin, with the front rather than the side of his cerebellum, or that some poems and novels were written when the leg of the author was callow while his arm or navel was ripening. I don't know what maturity means; perhaps it is another word for shrewd. No matter; if a man is wise, he is only so at moments, and for the most part he is puerile and his faculties are vacant.

There is as much Delphic wind in Longinus as in Coleridge or Eliot. Obviously, Eliot paraphrases Longinus's remark that a fine prose style is the "last fruit of long experience." But the ancient rhetorician affirmed that Homer's best work is the *Iliad* and that the *Odyssey*, the later poem, represents the bard's senilia.

There is no time in which man can be said to come to his senses: Euripides was of the mind that man is now good, and then bad, and he is almost always stupid. One philosopher told men that at some juncture in their lives they ought to trust themselves, but any russet bumpkin might ask when.

[148

It is now essential not only to inquire whether literary criticism is possible, but how it can be useful; and Longinus is enormously helpful in understanding the modern dilemma in letters. Tate asserts that "the literature of the present begins . . . with Homer." Were Rhadamanthus judging literature he could not have made a more just observation. As Tate extinguishes the past without being pedantic about it, some mention should be made of the academic who regards anyone who can go back as far as Henry James an antiquarian.

Since Tate believes that all ages are now, he deals with *On the Sublime* as a present-day oration on letters. In so doing, he quotes Longinus in order to dispose of the empty Bacchic furies of the lyrical novelist, and in particular Thomas Wolfe, the overstuffed cyclops of American dithyrambic fiction. He exhumes a wry perception from Longinus for this purpose: "Some writers fall into a maudlin mood and digress from their subject into their own tedious emotion. Thus they show bad form and leave their audiences unimpressed: necessarily, they are in a state of rapture, and the audience is not."

Although Tate argues that Aristotle could not know anything about the novel, I believe what Aristotle and Longinus have said about poetry is also the best criticism of this newer form. Tate declares that Longinus repeats Aristotle's caveat against the emphasis on "character," which Aristotle seems to think need not be much developed if the "plot" is good. The novelist generally is most sublime, as Longinus would have it, when he is a very good narrator: "the sublime is often found where there is no emotion."

Every classical critic from Aristotle, Longinus, Dryden, Coleridge, Hazlitt, to Herbert Read and Allen Tate, is sure, in attempting to capture the vaporous afflatus of the poet, to use ass's bladders to catch the Etesian gales. In an essay that has much insight, Tate maintains that "Our multiverse has increasingly, since the seventeenth century, consisted of unstable objects dissolving into energy; and there has been no limit to the extension of analogy." When he declares that Aristotle was not less intelligent than a modern critic, is he not loading his back with that sack of chaff called progress? Do we not have a penury of similes and words compared with a rural century? We live in a mechanical bedlam of the same drab objects, and fewer of them, so that the quantity of words required to describe them has dwindled enormously. In one lovely verse Tate has written: "Heredity/ Proposes love, love exacts language, and we lack/ Language." In another he writes:

> In the beginning the irresponsible Verb
> Connived with chaos whence I've seen it start
> Riddles in the head for the nervous heart
> To count its beat on . . .

As for energy what need of that has the megalopolitan clodpate who has been furnished with a college jargon to take the place of thought and an automobile to take him everywhere while he can be motionless and utterly lumpish? Man waxes pensive as he saunters, or is, as Aristotle claimed, most meditative when he is peripatetic; but then, the inert auto embryo can travel without walking and can be more stupid than the mole or the shrew.

Longinus also says that "most important of all, we must learn from art the fact that some elements of style depend upon nature." This would be a drossy conceit did not Longinus explain "nature," which he tells us "takes the place of good luck, and art, of prudent conduct." Chance is the wisest deity of the poet. When he happens to come upon an unusual simile or word it is unexpected. But here I think Tate is clearer than Longinus: "style comes into existence only as it discovers the subject . . . and the subject exists only after it is formed by the style."

In his essay, "Johnson on the Metaphysical Poets," Allen Tate takes Samuel Johnson to task. I believe no one has misliked Dr. Johnson so much since William Hazlitt as Allen Tate. How much of Johnson's *Lives of the Poets* is useful and sound I cannot even surmise. It would be cant on my part if I did not own that I have not reread the *Lives* for a lustrum; but were I to examine every volume that a critic analyzes or carps at, I should be as feeble and blind as Lamech. I must needs pore over a work many times even to retain a few lines; Donne remarks "but I find it true after long reading I can only tell you how many leaves I have read." Again we are strongly prompted to study the poem instead of the gloss upon it.

I found the *Lives* exceedingly entertaining, but then Johnson is a pedlar of gossip no less than Pepys, or Evelyn, or Diogenes Laertius, and, as Tate believes, the life is in the poem. What concerns us here are Johnson's pronouncements; one example that Tate uses comes from the life of Cowley. Upbraiding the metaphysical poets, Johnson claims: "Nor was the sublime more within their reach than the pathetic; for they never attempted that comprehension and expanse which at once fills the whole mind, and of which the first effect is sudden astonishment, and the second rational admiration. Sublimity is produced by aggregation, littleness by dispersion." Analyze this "hydra of discourse"— Ben Jonson's phrase. What, for instance, can one make of such a carcass adage as "sublimity is produced by aggregation, littleness by dispersion"? It cannot be translated into words that would help a poet compose an elegy or a reader hear an iambus with more feeling. Besides, why should poetry be sublime, or pathetic? Cannot it be as amative or gnomic as Donne or Theognis? Then would the "aggregation" of a thousand commonplaces put into Job's or Milton's balance weigh enough to amount to the sublime?

There is Johnson's other complaint against the metaphysical poets: "they never attempted that comprehension and expanse that fills the whole mind, and of which the first effect is sudden astonishment, and the second rational admiration." How can a writer endeavor to attain a "comprehension and expanse that fills the whole mind"? Assuming that this is comprehensible, and that the poet can be filled with the Kosmos when he is plying his meters, how does he really know whether he is not vacant, and has only succeeded in scambling up many emotions that result in "littleness by dispersion"?

Tate reminds us that Longinus did not oppose the "sublime" to the "little." However, the more we ponder Johnson's costive lucubration, the less likely are we to know, as Tate says, a "syllogism from a handsaw." And we have another slice of Johnsonian diction in the following that Tate cites: "These writers who lay on the watch for novelty, could have little hope of greatness; for great things cannot have escaped former observation. *Their attempts were always analytic; they broke every image into fragments; and could no more represent, by their slender conceits and laboured particularities, the prospects of nature, or the scenes of life, than he who dissects a sunbeam with a prism can exhibit the wide effulgence of a summer noon.*" "Up to the last sentence," alleges Tate, we have about "half of the ghost of Longinus." But the whole of this syntax could have been composed by Martin Scriblerus. When Dr. Johnson tries to bring off a poetic trope, the reader has a phlebotomy. If we iterate Johnson's phrases, "laboured particularities," "the prospects," or the "scenes of life," and "he who dissects a sunbeam with a prism can exhibit the wide effulgence of a summer noon," we have a farrago of platitudes and a ridiculous figure of speech.

Samuel Johnson mused a great deal upon the metaphysical poets, and Tate offers us another excerpt from the *Lives*: Johnson declares "they neither copied nature nor life; neither painted the forms of matter nor represented the operations of intellect." If these *perverse* bards refused to imitate nature or life, and declined to recognize the existence of matter, what were they doing? Had Johnson thought that the poets were depicting experience that was preterhuman, or not just the average, empiric life, we cannot believe that he, an acolyte of the ancients, could have passed over Aristotle's commentary: "we only represent men either better than they actually are, or worse, or exactly as they are; just as, in painting, the pictures of Polygnotus were above the common level." In the *Poetics* it is stated: "Homer has drawn men superior to what they are; Cleophon, as they are."

Should this quotation from Aristotle be beside the point, then I must admit, with the same candor and lack of nonsense that Allen Tate, with disarming charm, admits: "I confess that I do not understand what I have just written." No matter; I am unable to halt, and must ask what Johnson means when he claims that the metaphysical poets did not "represent the operations of intellect." No matter what these poets were doing, they were employing their minds.

Then there is the matter of Johnson's taste in literature; Tate takes the following stanza written by Abraham Cowley, which Johnson regarded as a paradigm of good verse:

> Several lights will not be seen,
> If there be nothing else between.
> Men doubt because they stand so thick i' the skie,
> If those be stars which paint the Galaxie.

Of the last two lines Tate holds that Dryden could have gotten them off in a fit of absent-mindedness, and that "but for the extra syllable in the fifth foot of the third line, [they] could have been written by Pope in a moment of fatigue."

That we are still gulping down these stale gammons of apothegms is doleful evidence of the pitiable worth of the human brain. At this point I must perforce take the hazard of asserting that Samuel Johnson had resolved to be great and thought he could attain it by employing a bloated syntax. Hazlitt, describing the elder Seneca while thinking of Johnson, says that Seneca would eat only horse-plums and pond-apples, and that he kept a giantess for his mistress. Tate, worried by his own acerbity, feels he has been too rough with Johnson. Nobody likes to cudgel a rogue until the witnesses themselves can no longer rejoice in the spectacle, and Johnson was not a villain.

Johnson's pietism lay heavy upon his constitutional phlegm; the devotional verse of secular poets seemed to have soured him the more. He thought that Donne's religious poetry was not the same as the prophet's; he never mentions Christopher Smart's "The Song to David," an astonishing poem. He should have been mindful of Owen Felltham who said: "Mee thinkes the reading of *Ecclesiastes*, should make a *Puritane* undresse his braine, and lay off all those *Phanatique toyes* that gingle about his *understanding*." Tate writes: "But what Johnson actually says is that religious contemplation is not a subject for poetry; and this is nonsense." "What was Johnson doing with St. John of the Cross, the poems of St. Thomas of Aquinas, . . . with the Psalms of David?"

It is hard to know when Johnson was religious or just shrewd. He was obligated to the forty-three booksellers who had engaged to pay for the

153]

publication of the *Lives of the Poets*, and hesitated to include Donne because he had not enough of a "reputation." Johnson showed not a pittance of kindness to the mad, indigent singer in Fleet Street, Christopher Smart, whose poems had a niggish market value. His remark, "and I'd as lief pray with Kit Smart as anyone else," is brass upon our palates. The pious Dr. Johnson so disliked another Christian, Dean Swift, that he could not allow that the latter wrote *The Tale of a Tub*. But then who is so uncharitable as a Christian? He could be such a beadle that he blamed Dryden and Pope for dedicating works to Congreve because the latter, though a master in the use of the English idiom, was a profligate. Nor must we overlook the trashy apocrypha about Richard Savage.

Has not the best criticism come from the poets themselves? Is not Milton's invocation to a felicitous accident far superior even to Longinus's homily on good fortune: "So may som gentle Muse/ With lucky words favour my destin'd Urn." And what need have we of Dr. Johnson's phlegmatic periods about novelty when we can find it in George Chapman's *Bussy D'Ambois* — "innovation is more gross than error"?

Perhaps Samuel Johnson was a great man; he was certainly a drumbling one. However, he deserves a high place among authors who are often just wise fools. He, like Silenus's ass, should be placed among the stars. That I have not done justice to Tate's eloquent theoretical argument with Dr. Johnson I know, but then I am writing a commentary on his gloss, and the best I can hope to do is to induce the reader to go straightway to Allen Tate's essay "Johnson on the Metaphysical Poets."

Edgar Allan Poe is the most baffling of all American writers; until I had studied the essays of Tate on Poe and Dante, I had not understood the immense importance of Poe's genius. Nor was I able to move from the works of Poe to the poems of Charles Baudelaire, his disciple. My views on Poe were "stumps of heresy."

Poe is indeed a perplexing sorcerer; he is a master of bathos — an oxymoron, I know. His *Marginalia,* as Tate has declared, is filled with "sham erudition." Tate also says Poe wrote of the abstruse books that Ligeia possessed, but which never existed. Yet Poe read. What books he reaped had an enormous effect upon him. It is quite conceivable that a man of genius like Edgar Poe should have had so much veneration for learning without possessing it, and yet be in some way a charlatan.

What then did he read? The *Tales*, occult syllogisms, were of the royal blood, as all genius is. That the following remarks are grounded upon conjecture must be admitted: the *Tales* were the children of Dante's *Inferno*, and the witchcraft in Poe may have come out of Increase Mather's *Remarkable Providences*. This scholarly author, dismissed, or not even known, because he was a warped Puritan, was perhaps the Cave of Endor for Edgar Poe. What knowledge Poe required for his funeral bedchambers, vaults, sepultures he may have come upon in this astonishing volume.

Allen Tate thinks that Poe read the *Pensées*, and I quote this passage Tate takes from Pascal which he believes explains in part Poe's attitude toward the universe. "The slightest movement affects the whole of nature." Interpreting Poe's *The Power of Words*, Tate claims: "It almost seems as if Poe had just read this passage and had come at once to his desk to begin *The Power of Words*." "One more step, and the 'slightest movement,' a spoken word, will act creatively": the word, concludes Tate, is "beautiful and hallowed, unless, of course, the *word* is a 'magic recipe,' incantatory magic, which I believe undoubtedly we get in *The Power of Words*." The savant of the *Pensées* was, at moments, in some adage or thought a Chaldean necromancer.

But words, like good counsel, have no effect upon unalterable character, and certainly none on the Kosmos. Is it idle to remark that papyrus grows in the shallows of the shoals? Let us return to the perplexity: after quoting a dialogue between Poe's Oinos and Agathos, Tate resumed his argument: "How had Agathos created this beautiful but unhallowed object? By the 'physical power of words,' he tells Oinos."

For one thing, the universe is indifferent to the *Iliad*; it too will perish and be forgotten. Whether Poe shuffled through some pages of the *Pensées* or not I do not know, and that is a certainty. But it is my guess, and let the scholars determine whether I am right or wrong, that he ransacked *Remarkable Providences* for what he needed.

Increase Mather could have furnished him with great references he did not have to acquire himself. On the pages of the *Remarkable Providences* were allusions to Sir Thomas Browne, Robert Burton, Dioscorides, Hesychius, Ovid, obviously read and cherished by Increase Mather, but loot for a man of letters who wants to be a sage. Poe was a genius whose awe of knowledge was as great as that of the ancient Jews, who could not see God face to face, but were told that if they looked upon his hinder parts they could be prophetic.

Let me assume that the reader is familiar with the *Tales* and that I need no more than refer to Poe's gaudy, funeral decorations, or what Tate calls the "machine of symbols," and he may then discern the influence of the *Remarkable Providences* on Poe. That we are dealing with satanism, magic, sorcery, should be evident to any serious advocate of Poe.

One can imagine how quick Poe would have been to pounce upon the following excerpt from Mather: "Especially it is true concerning melancholy, which has therefore been called Balneum Diaboli"; the *Tales* are a lamentation garnished with magic and witchcraft, which he took, at least in part, from Dante and Increase Mather. Of course, I do not know. The reader is entitled to plain words, and no shuffle, and so I shall take a few examples out of Mather's learned and neglected book, and then let the reader make his own decision:

It is no less superstitious when men endeavor by character, words, or spells, to charm away the witches, devils, or diseases.

There cannot be greater vanity than to imagine that devils are really frighted with words and syllables.

Saint Francis caused the devil to depart out of a possessed person by using an alike brutish expression. He folded up the paper in a cloth, requiring the diseased party to wear it about her neck.

whoso shall read Proclus his book, de Sacrificio et Magia, will see how the Ethnicks taught that smells and smokes would cause daemons to depart.

Porphyrius saith that the Egyptians had symbols which Serapis appointed them to use in order to the driving away daemons.

Nor can we fail to think of "The Fall of the House of Usher" as we muse upon this line: "some . . . advised the poor woman to stick the house round with bayes as an effectual preservative against the power of evil spirits." Poe's passionate concern with satanism and necromancy is so obvious that had Mather lived at the time Poe composed the *Tales,* he would have added the name of the American satanist to the list of demons mentioned in the Bible. Mather writes: "Scripture makes particular mention of many that used those cursed arts . . . that is, Jannes, and Jambres, Balaam, Manasseh, Simon, Elymas." Consider also Poe's raven and then ponder this line from *Remarkable Providences*: "De la Cerda speaketh of a crow that did discourse rationally; undoubtedly it was acted by a caco daemon."

It is also possible that Poe first came upon Glanvill in the book by Mather, and that he may have read Webster's book on witchcraft mentioned by that learned author. Is it necessary to mention the celebrated quotation Poe took from Glanvill and used in Ligeia? Also, are not the chambers and the house of Usher, tombs at Gadarene, inhabited by demons?

Nor is it ridiculous to compare Poe with Dante. Obviously, Poe as an author is only a caitiff angel from Dante's *Inferno.* Poe borrowed his sloughs, fens, loathsome pools, and marshes as well as his furies clothed in miasmas and the effluvia of scummed lakes from Dante. Says Tate: "Poe's heroines — Berenice, Ligeia, Madeline, Morella . . . are all ill-disguised vampires — his heroes necromancers . . . whose wills, like the heroines' wills, defy terms of life to keep them equivocally 'alive.'" "Poe's imagination," asserts Tate, "can be located in only two places in Dante's entire scheme of the after-life: in Canto XIII the harpies feed upon the living trees enclosing the shades of suicides — those 'violent against themselves'; in Canto XXXII we are in 'the Ninth Circle, where the doleful shades were sounding with their teeth like storks.'"

Dante searched for the light of God, Poe for a satanic flame. Dante's

157]

invocation is: "Turn, Beatrice, turn those holy eyes." According to Tate: "Poe's strange fire is his leading visual symbol . . . You will see it in the eye of the Raven; in 'an eye large, liquid, and luminous beyond comparison,' of Roderick Usher; . . . in 'Those eyes! those large, those shining, those divine orbs,' of the Lady Ligeia."

In one respect Poe sees more than Dante; the divine Italian poet portrays an allegorical purgatorio in which muddied shadows speak. But what is allegory in Dante is in Poe a reality in the world of the dead. Poe imagined that the deceased bones have motions and sensations. The "animated dead," Tate calls them in one of his poems. We do not know, as Tate claims, whether Ligeia, Madeline Usher, Morella, and Berenice are alive or dead, whether they have been annihilated by their lovers or have killed themselves. Returning to Increase Mather, we see that these Medusas are perhaps subject to syncope. They are the "undead," as Tate speaks of them. Poe was always meditating upon the experiences of the deceased; he was dealing with souls rather than with bodies; the corporeal heroes and heroines are undecayed, but the spirits are dead and corrupt matter, or, as Mather might have put it, they are under the influence of a deliquium.

Other comparisons between Dante and Poe are worth noticing; both poets were palmers making the hapless and impossible pilgrimage to the Empyrean, the habitation of Essences. Poe in *Eureka*, and in some of the *Tales*, as Tate states, fell into the "angelic fallacy." A universal or godhead sitting upon the summit of Mt. Ida, is ungraspable. Tate, alleging that neither Dante nor Poe can behold essences, adds: "If we take nothing with us to the top but our emptied, angelic intellects, we shall see nothing . . . Poe as God sits silent in darkness" and so does every metaphysician. Allen Tate claims that only angels, and not man have immediate knowledge of Absolutes. "Not," says Beatrice to Dante, "that such things are in themselves harsh; but on your side is the defect, in that your sight is not yet raised so high."

Poe, momentarily, recognized man's intellectual impotence; he writes: "Even while he stalked a God in his own fancy, an infantine imbecility came over him." Poe knew this in one essay or fable but not in another, and his pursuit of essences maimed his natural understanding of what Tate calls the "common thing." As a result of this we find in Poe's writing the fusty triad of the schoolmen, namely, feeling, intellect, and will. Tate declares: "Thus we get the third hypertrophy of a human faculty: the intellect moving in isolation from both love and the moral will, where it declares itself independent of the human situation." Lest we imagine that Tate thinks we are able to apprehend such operations of the will or the emotions apart from the intellect, he continues: "It is important . . . to observe that Poe takes for granted the old facultative psychology of intellect, will, and feeling." This triune has given us a turbid language; we know where the pinch lies, and yet when we endeavor to divide what appears to be various kinds of responses in people, we run upon the pikes. No one, not even Herbert Read, whose English is an ore of Ophir, is able to eschew such words as spirit and eternal verities. I suppose the best we can do about it is to accept Donne's explanation: "I say again, that the body makes the Minde." Otherwise, when we babble about reason, as something apart from sensibility, it is lofty prating.

Should there be any doubt of what Allen Tate says, more citations from Dante will truss up his true insights: here are the "shadowy prefaces" of Ligeia, Morella, Monos, and Una, "where all at once had raised up the Hellish Furies, stained with blood, who had the limbs and attitude of women." In the *Inferno* it is written: "the diviners, the augurs, sorcerers, coming slowly along the bottom of the Fourth Chasm. By help of their incantations and evil agents, they had endeavoured to pry into the Future which belongs to the Almighty alone." "We now arrived in the deep fosses, which moat that joyless city" of the *Inferno,* relates Dante, which introduces us to the House of Usher. Whether Berenice's lover extracted her teeth, or the latter is also a symbol of suicide, Poe may well have been thinking of "At Filippo Argenti! The passionate Florentine spirit turned with his teeth upon himself."

Allen Tate has said that the hearse-like furniture of Poe's stories is trumpery; instead of perception Poe gives us funeral appointments; Tate observes: "His purpose in laying on the thick decor was to simulate sensation." Unless we comprehend the reason for the trashy gothic ornaments in the *Tales* we are reading Poe without purpose. Again, Tate says: "but no man is going to use so much neo-Gothic over and over again, unless he means business with it."

Aristotle asserts that the use of such decorations shows a want of art. If we take Poe as an American magian instead of an unusual prose stylist, which he was not, we then see that in all the crepuscular furnishings, the bedchambers which are vaults or crypts, Poe gave us not the divine poetry of the nine circles, but mortuary tinsel, and rubbishy fantasies. In Poe we have diabolism, which, to quote Tate, is the privation of light, or as Dante says: "I am in the Third Circle, that of the eternal accursed, cold and heavy rain."

Poe was not concerned with sordid living bodies or their turgid senses; Tate declares: "Very rarely he gives us a real perception because he is not interested in anything that is alive. Everything in Poe is dead: the houses, the rooms, the furniture, to say nothing of nature and of human beings."

Why is it, as Tate observes, that there are no amours between the Po-esque lovers? There is incestuous passion between Roderick and Madeline Usher, but no sexual connection. Are the "undead" women succubae who have carnal intercourse with men when they are asleep? Was this in Poe's mind, there is reason to assume that, unlike the ancients, he did not associ-ate sleep with death. However, after the act of coition, the soul lags and sullenly throbs with a dull hypochondria. There is something of the can-ticle of the worm involved in erotical communion. When sensations are too acute flesh is well nigh dead; of such unendurable raptures we have these lines from Baudelaire's "Correspondences" translated by Allen Tate:

> Amber and myrrh, benzoin and musk condense
> To transports of the spirit and the sense!

Only Baudelaire came closer than Allen Tate to the enigma of the *Tales*. Crying out of the deepest abyss of man Baudelaire sighs: "Les morts, les pauvres morts, ont des grandes doleurs." The shrieks of the "troop of the undead," Tate's startling insight, are more terrible than the *planch*, the song of lamentation, of Dante's half-buried sinners. The heir of Poe understood his master's genius and believed that nobody, after his ambulatory life beneath the sun is finished, is totally dead. The bones, deprived of diction, sensibility, conceptions, and understanding, are still in motion and still dream. Lacking sight and touch, but containing some minute fragment of its former senses, the cadaver "lives." Or, as Tate writes in "The Ancestors": "The bones hear but the eyes will never see."

Constantly thinking about the miseries of the deceased, whose bones are unconscious but groan, Poe seemed indifferent to the canicular days of wretched man who lives. There is not one figure in Poe's *Tales* who, like Glaucus, even tastes the grass. Tate refers to the women in Poe as "undead" ladies and "machines of sensation."

The women in Poe are sorceresses, occult sibyls wholly aloof from the flock-bed and the midden. Ligeia, Berenice, and Madeline Usher seem to have walked out of Dante's pages: "See the wretched women who left the needle, the shuttle, the spindle, and made themselves divineresses; they wrought witchcraft with herbs and images."

For Poe does not see the talons of death tearing the countenances of the loved ones, their flesh and raiment still whole; his disciple, Baudelaire, however, embraces the madonna while she rots in his arms. This mordant knowledge of woman is our tragedy; we have been hoarse for centuries, and have no other amorous flame within us.

"A Carrion," englished by Tate, and just about the only translation of Baudelaire I have been able to read with pleasure, shows us our modern Helen as Poe's sublime worm fondled by his pupil:

> Speak, then, my Beauty, to this dire putrescence,
> To the worm that shall kiss your proud estate,
> That I have kept the divine form and the essence
> Of my festered loves inviolate!

"A Carrion" helps us to understand the quasi-deceased in Poe's *Tales*, those who are walled up, or interred, and abhorred and loved. The hero sepulchres his beauty, but does not quite murder her, nor does she altogether do away with herself. Dante had it: "Their covers were all raised up; and out of them proceeded moans so grievous that they seemed indeed the moans of spirits and wounded."

There is, among other difficulties I cannot resolve, another *dubbio*, a baffling question, in Poe's works. Why do the heroes desire to see the heroines dead? This is not just necrophilism; the clue is in the sentence selected by Tate, and taken from *Eureka*: "In the original unity of the first thing lies the secondary cause of all things, with the germ of their inevitable annihilation." Poe, as Tate alleges, was preoccupied with the catastrophe of the universe; this theme, "a cataclysmic end of the world, modeled on the Christian eschatology," in Tate's words, is in "The Conversation of Eiros and Charmion," "The Colloquy of Monos and Una," *The Power of Words*, and *Eureka*. What does, to cite Tate, this "semi-rational vision of the final disappearance of the material world into the first spiritual Unity, or God" signify? If I do not err, Poe could not endure his total separation from others which is man's portion and woe. Edgar Poe composed horror stories in which women are, perhaps, destroyed by their lovers whose appetites were not for their bodies, but for their souls or identities. Tate expresses it beautifully in his poem "Aeneas at Washington": "The singular passion/ Abides its object and consumes desire/ In the circling shadow of its appetite." Union with complete identification with another person is impossible, and that is a ludicrous statement; far closer to the truth and the tragic dilemma is that we don't know anybody, and are never able to *see* a face that belongs to somebody else or even our own.

Allen Tate remarks: "The theme and its meaning as I see them are unmistakable: the symbolic compulsion that drives through, and beyond, physical incest moves towards the extinction of the beloved's will in complete possession, not of her body, but of her being." This explains the infernal combat between Ligeia and her lover, between Madeline and Roderick Usher; each one is sorely wounded because of the intolerable gulf that divides them from each other. Tate writes: "The spirits prey upon one another with destructive fire which is at once pure of lust and infernal."

Poe only considered the joys of the body because they seemed to be so similar to the moods of buried bones; otherwise, as Tate has shown, Poe had no interest whatever in sensuality. Poetry is the terrain of the country, and neither Poe nor any other American poet has written amorous verse. Perhaps the closest we have come to the fires of Eros is in Allen Tate's marvelous translation of "The Vigil of Venus" (I cite here only one quatrain):

> Now the tall swans with hoarse cries thrash the lake:
> The girl of Tereus pours from the poplar ring
> Musical change — sad sister who bewails
> Her act of darkness with the barbarous king!

Or in this stanza from his poem "Seasons of the Soul":

> All the sea-gods are dead.
> You, Venus, come home
> To your salt maidenhead,
> The tossed anonymous sea
> Under shuddering foam —
> Shade for lovers, where
> A shark swift as your dove
> Shall pace our company
> All night to nudge and tear
> The livid wound of love.

At this point one must ask who besides the French symbolist poets and Allen Tate really understood the master of Baudelaire, Mallarmé, and Valéry? Poe has been dismissed as a scribbler of cheap gothic bathos, a nineteenth-century Cain who took laudanum and married a child who was thirteen years old. That he had few ideas, almost no sensibility or feeling, neither Tate nor anybody else who understands Poe can gainsay. But after one has said this, he still has misread the *Tales*. Aldous Huxley denounced Poe because his English is ungrammatical nonsense. Would it not be more intelligent to set aside the remarks of our well-known hackneys and turn to William Hazlitt, who said: "If I am assured that I never wrote a sentence of common English in my life, how can I know that this is not the case?"

By now it should be obvious that any real understanding of Poe hangs by the thread of Ariadne. Edgar Poe is simply nobody else, and we must let it go at that. Let us then endeavor to comprehend him as best we can. It won't do us any good if we imagine we can dismiss or undermine Poe by saying that "he had the tumours of a troubled mind," Milton's phrase. For above two thousand years and more, the poet has been looked upon as a putrescent biped with genius, utterly abnormal; but who can contemplate the average man, and consider his insane mechanical amusements, and not cower? Poe doubtless had most of the fevers and sick nerves of mediocre people, but he knew how to fable his malady. A banal man who is ill on top wishes to destroy everybody, a genius only craves to compose a book; he desires to make his illness useful to the commonwealth, or as Shakespeare tells us, "I will turn disease to commodity."

Notice should be taken of Poe's obsession with magic. Our Dr. Faustus was looking for a supernatural chemical, or syllable, that would give him power over nature. According to Tate, the American of that era viewed nature as the enemy: Moby-Dick is the lucifer swimming in the ocean seas, whose occult evil can never be overcome.

Whatever religious feeling Poe had I do not know; one might surmise that his heart bellowed until it burst its anguish, roaring, "My God, my God, there is no God!" He was deeply torn by kosmic apathy to human sorrow; the universe was the archfiend that ate man, and everything else it created. Maybe John Donne described Poe's attitude toward God: "It is a halfe *Atheisme* to murmure against Nature."

Poe is a colossus in any literature; he is, however, a gigantic dwarf with scarce any conceptions and with little human nature in him. An idea in the *Tales* is a sin against Poe's genius. Poe's demon was his fury rather than his parent, or as one Greek cynic has said: "For Zeus, father of us all, variously is father to some, to others but a step-father."

Of Poe Tate says: "The sensibility is frustrated, since it is denied its perpetual refreshments in nature." Poe has no sun or "lazy smoke" in his blood, and all of the erotic bouts between the dilacerated lovers take place on the livid shingle of Acheron.

At this point it is necessary for me to admit that I have been wrong